Sales Therapy®

Sales Therapy®

Effective Selling for the Small Business Owner

GRANT LEBOFF

CAPSTONE

Other Wiley Editorial Offices
John Wiley & Sons Inc., 111 River Street, Hoboken, NJ 07030, USA
Jossey-Bass, 989 Market Street, San Francisco, CA 94103–1741, USA
Wiley-VCH Verlag GmbH, Boschstr. 12, D-69469 Weinheim, Germany
John Wiley & Sons Australia Ltd, 42 McDougall Street, Milton, Queensland 4064, Australia
John Wiley & Sons (Asia) Pte Ltd, 2 Clementi Loop #02–01, Jin Xing Distripark, Singapore 129809
John Wiley & Sons Canada Ltd, 22 Worcester Road, Etobicoke, Ontario, Canada M9W 1L1
Wiley also publishes its books in a variety of electronic formats. Some content that appears in
print may not be available in electronic books.

Library of Congress Cataloging-in-Publication Data

Leboff, Grant.
  Sales therapy : effective selling for the small business owner / Grant Leboff.
    p. cm.
  Includes index.
  ISBN 978-1-84112-778-1
  1. Sales management. 2. Small business--Management. 3. Selling. 4. Customer relations. 5.
Relationship marketing. I. Title. II. Title: Effective selling for the small business owner.
  HF5438.4.L43 2007
  658.85--dc22

                                                                            2007030930

Anniversary Logo Design: Richard J. Pacifico

Set in ITC New Baskerville by Sparks, Oxford – www.sparks.co.uk
Printed and bound in Great Britain by TJ International Ltd, Padstow, Cornwall

This book is printed on acid-free paper responsibly manufactured from sustainable forestry
in which at least two trees are planted for each one used for paper production. Substantial
discounts on bulk quantities of Capstone Books are available to corporations, professional
associations and other organizations. For details telephone John Wiley & Sons on (+44)
1243–770441, fax (+44) 1243 770571 or email corporatedevelopment@wiley.co.uk

Contents

Moving Away from the Transactional Model

The old transactional sales model does not work any more

Compare the old transactional sales model with a car which has a worn out engine and is continually breaking down. Every few miles, you spend even more money on a quick fix so you can drive it a little longer. Really, you know that throwing money at it is a waste of time. However, without the wherewithal to replace it, you are unsure of the alternative.

The equivalent of this is happening in sales. People spend time re-hashing and re-inventing the old transactional sales model in order to try and squeeze out a few extra sales. All the while, people have instinctively understood that it really doesn't work.

Why, when people sell, do they:

- Still make 'sales presentations' when they are normally a waste of time?
- Still persist with the myth of 'open' and 'closed' questions, when the model is flawed?
- Still insist on 'selling the benefits' when they are ineffective?
- Still obsess with 'handling objections', when it is the traditional sales model that creates them?
- Still focus on 'closing' when that is not the way to get results?

Many business owners who need to sell, but who are not professional sales people, already feel uncomfortable with the old transactional sales model. They know they have to put the relationship with the client first; but do not have a model with which to achieve it.

The idea of the importance of the relationship is not new. The problem is that sales practitioners continue to use the transactional model and then pretend to make the relationship their utmost concern. This simply does not work.

However 'interested' these people try to look when they are with their customers, they still endeavour to press home their presentation, handle objections and sell the benefits. What they are really doing is trying to force a square peg into a round hole. This is transactional selling presented to look like the relationship is important.

The old model simply does not work.

- Sales Therapy® is a fresh approach to selling.
- The focus is on the customer; not on the sales person.
- The relationship comes first; not the transaction.
- The focus is on the sales process; not on the result.

Sales Therapy® will show you how to sell more naturally and commit your closing techniques to the recycle bin.

With this new approach to selling, a salesperson does not have to pretend they have all the answers. Like a therapist, they are there to ask the questions.

Sales Therapy® is therapy for both parties. The old adversarial boxing match, which selling so often becomes, is cast aside. In this new selling, both buyer and seller gain from the relationship and the discussion, whatever the outcome.

This does not mean we will not make sales. However, the sale is the transaction at the end of a process. The process is about the customer. It is about helping them.

In other words:

- Selling is not about achieving the salesperson's goals; but fulfilling those of the customer.
- It is not about making sales; but helping people buy.
- It is about concentrating on the process; not the outcome.

Every business owner has a commercial imperative. They need to make sales in order to stay in business. However, selling is 'win–win'; not 'win–lose'.

It is now necessary to cast the old models aside. We must recognize the dramatic changes we have all experienced in every aspect of our lives, with business being no exception.

Prior to the Industrial Revolution there were many small business owners. Village bakers, blacksmiths, ironmongers and cobblers traded within their local communities.

The Industrial Revolution changed all that. It put the means of production into the hands of the few. To compete in this new world required an enormous amount of capital investment. Expensive machinery, large factories, an efficient supply chain and distribution channels were all essential. Therefore, the average worker found themselves employed by someone else.

We are now living in a post-industrial era. It is no longer necessary to work for others; today's technology does not require a large capital outlay to start a business. You can purchase a laptop and a mobile phone, print a few business cards and be in business, trading from your front room, within a matter of hours.

In many ways, we have come full circle. There is now a proliferation of small businesses. There are over four million businesses in the UK; of these; approximately 99% have less than 50 employees. Over 70% have no employees at all. The majority of businesses, therefore, consist of only small business owners. This is not a trend exclusive to the UK. For example, the percentage of businesses consisting solely of small business owners is virtually the same in the USA.

Every one of these small entities has to promote itself. Whether companies are using direct mail, e-mail, telemarketing, networking, advertising, word of mouth marketing, or any of the other routes to market that are available, the net result of all this activity is more 'noise' in the market place than ever before.

This 'noise' crosses borders. Globalization means that companies are not only competing in their own back yard, but all over the world. Furthermore, we have seen the deregulation of certain markets such as telecoms and financial services. Globalization, the proliferation of small businesses and the deregulation of markets have created more suppliers, providing more products and services than in any previous generation. Competition is fiercer today than it has ever been. There is an old adage, 'The customer is king.' The reality of this was not always true. However, with the amount of choice the customer has today, this is now definitely the case. Consider the changes.

> Up to the early 1980s, if you needed a mortgage, you applied to your bank manager or building society with some trepidation. This was because if you were turned down, you were left with very few alternatives to fund a house purchase. Today, even if you are experiencing exceptional financial problems, there are innumerable mortgage companies vying for your business.

The same is true for personal credit; wherein banks, retailers and other businesses compete for customers to use their own card. It does not matter whether the market is financial services, utilities, cars, restaurants or TV channels. There is more competition than ever before, giving customers an increasing amount of choice.

Not only do consumers have more choice, but they are also more knowledgeable. As the market place has matured, we have become increasingly sophisticated buyers. We have ever greater access to information. A major contribution to this phenomenon is the meteoric growth of the Internet which enables buyers – private or business – to research and compare companies and products in minutes. It wasn't too long ago that if you wanted to source a product or service there was little choice other than to consult trade publications or Yellow Pages. Now you can search on the Internet and find a supplier without even leaving your desk. We can obtain what we want, when we want it, from virtually anywhere in the world.

> This new customer freedom was utilized almost immediately. In the days when the Internet was still relatively new to most people, the media got hold of the story that British customers were paying far higher prices for their vehicles than their counterparts in mainland Europe. British consumers started to use the Internet to purchase their cars abroad, making large savings. This forced a review of the prices that UK companies were charging. The ability to compare prices and source product overseas changed the rules by which we all operated. Suddenly, the consumer had a control that had never previously been conceived.

The market place is crowded. In a market full of suppliers, power lies with the consumer. This means that business has to invest more time and money in order to win new customers.

In short, acquisition costs are going up.

Fierce competition means prices are not increasing at the same rate. In fact, in many market sectors they are being driven down. For a business to acquire a customer and make one transaction does not make sense. It does not produce enough profit. Because companies have to invest more money to acquire their customers, the value of a customer's order must increase as well. Suppliers cannot afford to focus on one transaction. They have to look at the lifetime value of a customer. For example:

> A car dealership does not want to just sell the car. They want to sell the car, the extras, servicing and, when the car is due for replacement, they want that customer to purchase from them all over again. Furthermore, the dealer wants that customer to recommend them to family and friends.

In other words, the emphasis in today's business climate has moved away from making transactions to building relationships.

The key to success is putting the relationship first; the transactions then follow. The traditional model of selling, however, is a transactional one. It simply does not allow for this to happen.

REPUTATION

No company ever wants to have a bad reputation. Years ago, when a company may have had only one or two competitors, it could often survive despite its shortcomings. With limited choices, and restricted access to knowledge, it was inevitable that some customers would end up using the company; almost by default. However, this is no longer the case. Businesses are operating in fiercely competitive markets, where customers have a plethora of choices. Reputation is now a fragile and valuable asset.

A good reputation will help you to rise above the crowd. A bad reputation could kill you.

In the old world, when we had a bad experience we would tell a few people. Eventually, we would get bored of recounting our tale and the story would be forgotten. Today, not only will we tell some of our closest friends and colleagues, but it is possible that we will e-mail or text our entire address book. Moreover, if we feel particularly aggrieved we may choose to post a blog on the Internet. Consider the full impact of the following personal experience:

> I attended a breakfast meeting in a London hotel where a lady, who had recently flown in from the United States, was staying. On meeting her for the first time, she seemed particularly angry. I naturally asked her what was wrong, whereat she recounted her previous two miserable days in this particular establishment. She finished her story with the words; 'and I am going to blog the hell out of this hotel when I get back home'. Sure enough, when I last checked, if you search for the hotel's name, her blog, airing all her grievances, still comes up on the same page as the hotel.

Although she must be a total stranger to practically everyone who reads it, I cannot imagine anybody booking a room there after reading the contents of her blog. No longer will her complaining stop when she gets bored of recounting her experiences. Her complaint has been posted on the web with the potential to damage that hotel's business for many years to come. In today's climate, companies simply cannot afford to mis-sell, make empty promises or let their customers down.

The emphasis has moved from the transaction to the relationship.

Focusing on the transaction means putting the transaction first. What is of utmost importance is getting the deal. This can lead to mis-selling or overselling, whereby, in order to get the business, you may raise the customer's expectations so much that they can only be left disappointed later on.

If you put the relationship first, this is unlikely to happen because your priority is your customer. Their interests come first; everything else is secondary. This approach will mean you are more likely to retain and enhance your good reputation. With the dissemination of information available and word of mouth recommendations, a good reputation will ultimately lead to more sales.

THE CHANGING BUSINESS CLIMATE

It is clear there is a problem with sales today.

Changes in the world have rendered the old transactional sales model obsolete.

Yet most books on sales, sales training courses and sales departments still use this model, albeit often disguised in different language. It simply defies logic that businesses have evolved beyond all recognition, yet the sales model has not changed at all. Consider some of the operational changes companies have had to make:

- An increasing amount of processes have been automated, using technology, in order to increase efficiency and speed. This has led to dramatic changes within organizations and means that IT is now integral to business strategy.
- Many organizations now outsource key aspects of their operation, which they would never have previously considered outsourcing.
- Other companies have offshore operational departments, whereby a customer based in London may be serviced by someone in another country.

Furthermore, companies have not only had to change operationally; changes have taken place right across the spectrum. Another example would be Human Resource departments:

- As we have become wealthier, money is no longer the only consideration when attracting and retaining staff. Other benefits and quality of life issues are also taken into account by employees.
- As the global employee market becomes more competitive, there is an increasing emphasis on training and development within companies.
- There is also a greater merging of home and business life, as technology means people don't have to be behind their desk to achieve results. Mobile phones and laptop computers mean people can be productive in a variety of places at times that suit them.

So, why is it, when there have been such enormous changes to the way we conduct business, people treat sales as if it has never changed?

There is now a mismatch between how people behave when selling and all other aspects of business. It beggars belief that so much has changed in the world, but the sales model has not changed at all. The traditional sales model has remained in a vacuum as the world of commerce has moved on.

Selling Snow to the Eskimos

'He can sell snow to the Eskimos'

Is this selling or is this fraud?

This well-known phrase is often used to describe a great sales person; the idea being that this person can even sell something the recipient does not require; but is that really what selling is all about? In a world where relationships and reputation are so important, this attitude can cause significant damage to any business and yet the notion that the transaction takes priority and nothing else matters, still persists.

We need to appreciate that 'transactional' selling is so ingrained in our culture that it has become an unchallenged part of our language. This poses a very real problem because; if the very essence of selling is not properly understood, there is very little chance that the process will be carried out effectively. Despite this, the transactional model of selling is perpetuated throughout the world. This is highlighted in two leading English dictionaries; Merriam-Webster in the US and the Oxford English Dictionary in the UK. Both publish a variety of definitions for the verb 'sell', each according to different circumstances, yet the two similar definitions that are most relevant for our purposes are both transactional in nature.

DICTIONARY DEFINITION [I]

> *'give up to another for something of value'* (Merriam-Webster)

> *'hand over in exchange for money'* (Oxford English Dictionary)

To 'hand over in exchange for money' is not selling.

- It is the sale.
- It is the transaction.
- There is no reference here to any process.

If I give you a pen and you give me £1; that is to 'hand over in exchange for money' and this is how selling has always been seen. However, if you define your job as getting someone 'to hand over in exchange for money' then you make selling a 'zero sum game'. Either the customer 'hands over in exchange for money' or they don't. If they do, you win; if they don't, you lose.

Using this transactional definition, there is no recognition of the sales person adding value in any other way. The result is everything. In this scenario, the transaction has to be the primary objective of a sales person. By definition, the customer's interest is then of secondary consideration. Is it any wonder that sales people have a fear of rejection? In a 'zero sum game' they have so much to lose.

The transactional model of selling implies that sales people add no value other than obtaining a purchase at the end of a process. Therefore every interaction ever experienced with a customer has the potential to be win or lose. Make or break. Put into this context, it is no surprise that two commonplace occurrences happen when selling:

1   Sales people waste their time with customers who are never going to buy, but for one reason or another are reluctant to say no. In a

win or lose situation, a sales person is trying to avoid losing. They may not necessarily win, but they have not yet lost. The result is sales people who spend much of their time serving a pipeline that will never come to anything. This means, of course, that in the long run they will never generate a level of business of which they, or their company, will be proud.

2   Mis-selling and overselling take place. If someone is going to lose, human nature dictates that most sales people would prefer it to be the customer, not themselves. In today's climate this approach can be so damaging to a business.

This is where small business owners start to come unstuck.

A sales person in a large corporate can make a sale and receive a pat on the back from the sales director. Any mis-selling or overselling, which can result in the reputation of the company being damaged, often ends up as someone in the customer service department's problem and is no longer the responsibility of the individual sales person. Not only is this not moral, but in today's business climate it can be commercial suicide over a period of time. Nevertheless, the transactional model will often encourage this behaviour from a sales person who is often one step removed from the rest of the process.

Small business owners are much closer to the process.

When a customer complains, it will not be the phone in the customer service department that rings, but the business owner's. Therefore many business owners already have difficulty selling using the transactional model. The inherent problems that can get lost in a big organization stop right at the business owner's door. With the transactional model so prevalent, many business owners are left trying to muddle through on their own.

If we were to say that to 'hand over in exchange for money' is an acceptable definition of selling, it would make it one of the only professions in the world to define itself by the 'desired outcome'. This is ridiculous. Imagine what would happen if another professional, for example a doctor, were to do the same thing:

> A doctor who practises medicine could define their job as 'the treatment and prevention of disease'. This definition allows them to take a holistic approach. With a patient, it requires them to ask questions, undertake an examination, consider problems arising or additional relevant factors and as a result of that consultation, offer a treatment taken from a variety of different outcomes. For example, the doctor could send you home to get better; give you an injection; prescribe a medicine, such as big yellow tablets; send you for further tests; or, if unable to help, refer you to a specialist.

Now, let's see what happens when a doctor defines themselves by only one of the possible outcomes. In this example the doctor is no longer someone who treats and prevents disease but is now someone who 'prescribes big yellow tablets'. In many ways, asking questions and undertaking an examination is now superfluous, because the doctor already knows what he or she is going to recommend.

How often does a sales person make this mistake and fail to understand their customer? This is bound to happen when a sales person is merely going through the motions. Ultimately, the customer's answers are irrelevant to the sales person because they too already know what their recommendation will be. Their only reason for listening to a customer is to justify the position they already know they will take:

> So; you go to the doctor with a sore throat and the doctor prescribes 'big yellow tablets'. If you have a migraine, the doctor prescribes 'big yellow tablets'. Arthritis; 'big yellow tablets.' In fact, a doctor who defines themselves in this way has to prescribe 'big yellow tablets' whatever the symptoms, be it a broken leg or a suspected ulcer.

Now imagine that your doctor is paid commission on the number of 'big yellow tablets' prescribed. Who in their right mind will visit that doctor now?

Yet, this is the scenario that takes place as a result of the transactional model of selling. A sales person has a limited number of solutions at their disposal. They define their job **only** by getting customers to buy those solutions; rendering the customer's situation irrelevant. Meanwhile, the customer will be aware that the salesperson is being paid commission as a result of the transaction. Yet the sales person expects to gain the customer's trust. In reality, this is absurd.

DICTIONARY DEFINITION [II]

> *'persuade or influence to a course of action or to the acceptance of something' (Merriam-Webster)*

> *'persuade someone of the merits of ...' (Oxford English Dictionary)*

This is the archetypical vision of selling. It implies that a sales person approaches a potential buyer and, using 'the gift of the gab', attempts to convince or persuade that person, to do or buy something.

Many sales people feel more comfortable describing their occupation as persuading someone of the merits of their product or service. In this scenario, they are not driving a straightforward transaction; rather, undertaking a 'process of persuasion'.

However, whichever way you try to extrapolate it, this is still a transactional definition. The only reason I am trying to persuade my customer of something is so they will 'hand over in exchange for money.' There is simply no other point to the persuading. After all, if the sales person is successful in persuading the customer, they are not going to just walk away. The logical next step is for the customer to buy their product or service. Therefore, this definition still makes the transaction the most important aspect of the process. The persuading is undertaken solely to fulfil the aims of the sales person, which is to get the transaction. Once again, the customer's interests are secondary.

Sales Therapy® concludes that it is **not** the sales person's job to persuade the customer to do anything. A sales person, of course, cannot help but have some influence; but it should not be with the sole intention of getting the customer to accept their solution. It may be, however, that having engaged in a positive conversation, where options are explored, the customer might be persuaded or influenced to buy from the sales person.

Is this playing with semantics?

What is the difference between persuading someone, on the one hand, or them being persuaded or influenced, on the other?

The difference is one of **intent**.

In the dictionary definitions, the intention of the sales person is to persuade or influence **solely** for the purpose of achieving a transaction. This is not the case in Sales Therapy®. The transaction is of secondary concern. We engage in a good conversation with a potential customer, only to help them; not to coerce them into buying. A transaction will only take place if it is in the customer's best interest to do so; something only they should decide.

By targeting your efforts properly, you can ensure you have conversations with the people you are most likely to be able to help, and can therefore still make certain you are successful. Moreover, in a world where reputation is so important and dissemination of information so easy, the benefits of putting the customer first will outweigh any transactions lost by taking this approach.

A person who only deals with satisfied customers will, over time, receive many recommendations by word of mouth. These will increase when they also have a reputation for honesty. Recommendations will come even from the people who could not be helped. These people feel happy to recommend friends and colleagues to someone who they know will walk away from a transaction when it is not right for the customer.

The Sales Therapy® view is one where you empower and enable your customer to buy from you when it is in their interest to do so. With this approach, the emphasis moves away from selling and the traditional images it evokes; to one of facilitating the buying process.

The transactional view of selling, on the other hand, is one where the sales person puts their own interests first. This is not the most effective way to operate today.

Putting the
Relationship First

The transactional model of selling is endemic in our culture and has been the primary method of selling throughout the 20th century. Today, however, we need something different. We need a way of defining selling which allows the seller to put the relationship first. Sales Therapy® is this model and defines selling in two ways:

SALES THERAPY® DEFINITION [I]

'Problem Solving'

Every single purchase solves a problem:
Therefore, selling is about solving problems.

We make many everyday purchases to solve practical problems; for example:

We buy a pint of milk; otherwise we cannot have breakfast.

We buy petrol for the car; otherwise we cannot get from A to B.

These examples are easy to understand. However, as we become wealthier, we make fewer purchases based solely on practical considerations. Emotional sensibilities are often more important. In the main, the less mundane the purchase, the more prevalent emotional problems become. Because emotional problems are so personal in nature, they are less easy to identify. Even so, these problems are real and we must not make the mistake of forgetting their existence.

It is important to note that any problem has only to exist in the reality of the purchaser. Their perception, at the time, is the only one that matters. Whether anybody else believes the problem is real, is irrelevant.

To understand the variety of problems that can exist, let us take the example of buying a suit:

1   The problem is purely practical:

Joanne is required to wear a dark suit at her new place of work. However, she currently does not own one. She is unexcited by the prospect of the purchase and intends to do no more than to buy a suit to fulfil the requirement.

2   The problem is both practical and emotional:

Joanne looks to purchase a dark suit which she currently does not own, but is required to have at her new place of work. However, why is Joanne looking at buying an expensive, designer label? This purchase will solve the emotional problems of how she wants to be perceived by others (status) and how she perceives herself (aspirations).

3   The problem is purely emotional:

There can be an endless number of emotional problems that are solved with any one particular purchase. Below are some common examples:

- Joanne has nothing to do:

  So she goes shopping. For many people, shopping malls have become the 21st century theme parks. Just going shopping, in itself, solves a problem. Many retailers recognize this and an increasing number of shopping centres can be seen pampering to the requirement for activity displacement. Shopping centres, shop windows and displays are all designed to create desire and a feeling of 'missing out'. In these surroundings, people will often become dissatisfied with their current reality and spending a significant amount of time in this environment can stimulate a powerful desire to 'have'. The problem, then, becomes one of needing relief. This problem can only be resolved by making a purchase. What is bought is almost irrelevant. On this occasion, Joanne buys a dark suit.

- Joanne already possesses several dark suits:

  All of which would be suitable to wear at her new place of work. Yet, she goes shopping to buy another dark suit. Of course, there are a number of emotional problems this purchase could solve and the problem will vary depending on the person. Below are some possibilities:

  1 The problem of low self esteem:

     Joanne does not feel good about herself. She could buy anything today, but she has an excuse to purchase a new dark suit. The purchase allows her to feel good about herself, albeit only temporarily. The process of choosing and buying the new suit also gives her a sense of control in her life that she often lacks. (These emotions are partly why some people become addicted to shopping; the phenomenon known as retail therapy.)

  2 The problem of lack of confidence:

     Joanne is apprehensive about her new job. She feels that walking into her new office, wearing a brand new suit will make her feel good about herself and therefore give her extra confidence.

> 3 The problem of status and aspirations:
>   Joanne wants to walk into her new job in a brand new, fashionable suit. This solves the problem of how she will be perceived by her new employers (status) and how she perceives herself taking this new opportunity (aspirations).

There is another phenomenon: impulse buying:

It occurs frequently because more people today have the knowledge and economic means to take the inherent risk of making sudden purchases. The motivations behind these purchases will still be the same as for Joanne and her suit; only the timescales in which they are made will change.

As it is impossible to cover the plethora of problems that someone may be trying to solve, the examples given will show some of the possibilities. It is also important to understand that many of these problems will exist in combination with each other and do not fit conveniently into separate compartments. When selling, if you understand the problems the purchaser is trying to solve, you are more likely to make the sale.

We have several examples of Joanne buying a dark suit but, within these examples, her motivations for buying the suit are very different. In every one, the suit that Joanne eventually buys could plausibly be the same. It is the sales messages that will have to vary. Think about Joanne's priorities. They will be very different if she is purchasing the suit with purely practical considerations in mind as opposed to when her priorities are ones of status and aspiration.

The principle for the person selling never changes. Selling is about solving problems. If you can truly understand your customer's problem and have an appropriate solution, you have a good chance of making the sale.

SALES THERAPY® DEFINITION [II]

'Conveying Possibility'

Conveying possibility is a fundamental aspect of selling. You may have a product or service of which people have never heard or previously considered. They may not understand how your product or service could help their business or personal life and why it would justify the investment. As with therapy, by exploring ideas, you increase your customer's awareness. This may alter their perspective.

In order to do this, however, you have to be an expert. An effective sales person is, today, an educator and a teacher. They are extremely knowledgeable within their specialist area. This is because, when selling, your job is to show people what is available and what is possible. You are widening their horizons and explaining things to them in a language that they can understand.

This has become increasingly important in the world in which we live. The phenomenal pace of change, combined with the amount of choice we have, means that buying can often be extremely complicated. For example:

> Consider the purchase of a TV. Once upon a time the choice was colour or black and white. Now the choice is between LCD or plasma screens, and TVs fitted on the wall or sitting on stands. There is 5.1 surround sound and high definition technology available; all at vastly differing price points. Finding the appropriate TV is not as easy as it once was.

This is true for so many aspects of our lives.

Unless we are experts ourselves, we often need help in order to make our purchasing decisions. Ultimately, conveying possibility is about showing a customer the options they have at their disposal. It is about showing someone that there may be a better way of doing something. Of course, this may mean that there is no better way to be found, and if that is the case, you must be willing to walk away. Equally, if there is a better way, but one with which you cannot help, you must be willing to recommend an alternative solution.

This is selling with integrity.

Selling with integrity means: putting the customer first.

CONVEYING POSSIBILITY IS NOT A COP OUT

The idea that selling is just about showing a customer the options available can make it sound all too simple. In fact, if taken the wrong way, it could make selling sound like a type of information service whereby sales people do not really sell at all, but provide impartial information to customers. Of course, if this were the case, then surely the company providing the best product or service will be the only one that is recommended.

This is, of course, not the case. A sales person is not a passive information service. They are there to **pro-actively** convey possibility and help a customer solve problems. A passive attitude would mean that a sales person dispassionately provides information. Pro-active implies that they explore and are creative in finding a solution. For example, a customer calls a restaurant:

Passive response:

Customer: 'What meat do you serve?'

Restaurant Owner: 'Lamb and beef sir.'

Customer: 'Thank you. Goodbye.'

Pro-active response:

Customer: 'What meat do you serve?'

Restaurant Owner: 'Were you looking for anything in particular sir?'

Customer: 'We wanted to hire a private room for a turkey dinner.'

Restaurant Owner: 'How many guests will you party comprise sir?'

Customer: 'Fifteen guests.'

Restaurant Owner: 'That is no problem sir; we are happy to prepare a special turkey meal for 15 guests. What date do you want?'

In the first example, the restaurant owner takes the passive information service approach and does not get the business. In the second example, they take a pro-active, problem solving approach and get the business.

It will, therefore, be entirely appropriate for a person selling to recommend their own solutions. If they find they can never legitimately recommend their own product or service, there can only be two possible explanations:

1   Their product or service is not commercially viable (of course, any company without a commercially viable solution is doomed to fail); or
2   They are targeting entirely the wrong audience for the product or service they have.

It is unlikely, in the competitive world in which we operate today, that there is one product or service that should always be recommended.

For most customers, it is not about buying the best or the cheapest, but the most appropriate. Costs, timescales, specification, colour, geographical location, terms of delivery and many other factors will contribute to whether the particular product or service is right for a client. In any case, these terms are often negotiated in order to suit the customer's requirements because any company's standard terms and specifications may often not be entirely suitable.

A sales person will undoubtedly influence a potential customer, as will any thorough conversation about any given subject. As long as they genuinely put the customer first and are prepared to walk away if they cannot help, it is entirely appropriate that they recommend their solution when they believe it will help the customer. This, of course, requires a high degree of morality but in the transparent world in which we all live, to be effective in business, it is essential.

Conveying possibility presents other challenges. By showing some-one a better way of doing something, the implication is that whatever the customer is currently doing, is wrong. Although, when selling, you will not say this directly, it is a fact that is impossible to ignore. The two are mutually exclusive. If there is a better way, the inference is that whatever your customer is currently doing cannot be as good.

By conveying possibility, you are asking your customer to 'embrace new ideas'. This needs to be done delicately and depending on the experience and skill of the person selling, can result in very different outcomes. This is because 'embracing new ideas' means a customer has to move outside of their 'comfort zone'. In the main, this is some-thing none of us like to do, however small the risk:

Most of us will take the same route to work every day. We have become familiar with the roads, stations and traffic lights that we pass, along the way. We will also have our own routine; be it reading a newspaper on the train or listening to a particular radio station in the car. Think how uncomfortable, or even defensive you may feel, if a friend suggests a better route. Although it may save 20 minutes on your journey, it is something new. It introduces fears such as getting lost, venturing into unfamiliar places and having to alter the routine with which you have grown accustomed. In short, the thought of changing something so familiar is uncomfortable.

Moreover, if you have taken this journey to work for some considerable time, being made aware of a route which would save you 20 minutes every day could make you feel somewhat foolish.

In this example, no additional costs are involved and the recommendation has been made by a friend; yet you are still uncomfortable at the very thought of changing your routine. Moreover, you may even be tempted to justify the reason for taking that particular route. This will be done to prevent loss of face. After all, no one spends 20 minutes more every day on their journey to work if it is not necessary. This being the case, how difficult is it to accept a change that has been recommended by someone less familiar and when the stakes are higher?

Imagine a business owner who is running an efficient and profitable business. They have a meeting with a sales person who demonstrates a piece of software which will reduce their administration costs by £10,000 p.a. This should be good news. However, this software has been available for the last five years. Emotionally, if the business owner accepts that this software will help, then they have potentially wasted £50,000. How does this reflect on them?

Some business owners may readily embrace the new found opportunity; some may dismiss the sales person out of hand and decide the software must be 'too good to be true'; whilst other business owners may take this new information on board and explore the market further.

Conveying possibility is not a cop out or a vague concept. It is not easy to do. People do not like to feel vulnerable, or be told that they are wrong and they certainly do not like change. Conveying possibility often encompasses all three. Have you ever had a customer where your solution seemed so right and yet they would not buy? Conveying possibility demonstrates that there is more than logic involved in a buying decision. Only by understanding this can we start to deal with some of the problems that conveying possibility poses.

CREATING PROBLEMS

Selling is about problem solving. Every purchase solves a problem and, sometimes, by conveying possibilities, sales people create problems that they can solve. This is not manipulation. If the person selling always tells the truth, they cannot create problems that do not exist. They may, however, alert their customer to a problem they did not realize they had. In other words, the problem always existed, the customer was just not aware of it.

For example, our business owner who can save £50,000 on administration costs was unaware of this. They went to work that morning believing they had no problems in the administration department. Having met the sales person, they went home that evening burdened with the problem that their administration department was costing too much. The problem always existed; what changed was their awareness of it and the possibility that their competitors could already be using this software, potentially making them less competitive.

Even when a sales person has a formidable solution, as in our software example, conveying possibility works both ways. The person selling is there to show a customer there may be a better way; however, they must listen to the customer and have the integrity to walk away if they cannot help. For example, if our business owner is going to sell the company in the short term; investing in a new software program at that time, with all the upheaval it will create and the management time required for its implementation, would make the project totally inappropriate.

So selling is about solving problems. Sometimes customers will recognize the problems they have. Conveying possibilities, on these occasions, will be about finding the most appropriate solution for the customer. At other times, customers may be unaware of the problems that exist. By conveying possibilities, sales people create their own opportunities. By making a customer aware of a problem, they take the first step to finding an appropriate solution. Whatever the role of the sales person, in any particular circumstance, they should always conduct themselves with the utmost integrity. This is not just morally right, but, in today's business environment, it makes commercial sense.

The old transactional sales model does not allow room for integrity in selling, because it demands that sales people put the transaction first. This is what most sales people have been trained to do for generations. Nothing less than an order in their book is acceptable.

Sales Therapy® puts the customer first; you do not focus on the transaction at all. In fact it is quite the opposite; the transaction should be right at the back of your mind. When selling, a person's focus should only be on conveying possibility and solving problems. If selling is only about showing people there may be a better way and solving the problems they have, then selling, ultimately, is about nothing more than **helping people**.

Sales Therapy® recognizes that selling is about helping people. With this in mind, when selling you:

- no longer have to apologize for what you do;
- no longer have to fear rejection;
- no longer have to feel awkward because of the bad reputation that selling has previously had.

Selling is not about selling snow to the Eskimos; it never was. Selling is about focusing on the customer and helping them. If we do that properly, the transactions will occur naturally.

IS THIS COMMERCIAL SUICIDE?

Transactional selling and Sales Therapy® are the antithesis of each other. You cannot do both. For many sales people, the very idea of 'not focusing on the transaction' seems ridiculous. However, it is counter-intuitive.

You do not increase your sales by focusing exclusively on the transaction. The logic of this would be that if you are not selling, you are not focusing hard enough on the result. Many people in sales perpetuate this myth. If a sales person is struggling, we are often led to believe it is because they cannot 'close'. This thesis is risible. If someone does not want your product or service, it does not matter how hard you 'close' them. In a world where customers have immediate access to knowledge and a vast array of choice, if they do not want something, they will not take it. 'Closing' hard will just destroy any relationship you may have created earlier on. Similarly, 'closing' hard will not show the customer how you can solve their problems, what options they have and where the value in your solution lays. These aspects of a potential sale are developed long before the 'close'.

Not only does focusing on the transaction not guarantee success, but it will often prevent it. The sales person becomes so focused on getting the deal that they fail to develop the sale properly.

There is no doubt that in business there is a commercial reality with which we all have to live; however, focusing exclusively on commercial pressures is not the way to be most effective. If the sole focus is on the customer and gaining a full understanding of them, then sales will naturally take place. These will present themselves as solutions to a customer's situation. Thus, in Sales Therapy® the emphasis changes from making a sale to helping people buy. This approach is much more powerful and effective.

> Doctors focus solely on their patients and attempt to gain a full understanding of them during their consultation. They may not be able to help everyone, but in many cases, doctors will be able to prescribe a suitable remedy so as to make a visit to the surgery worthwhile. In the main, we trust doctors because their knowledge and professional manner tells us they are an expert. We also trust that if they cannot help, they will not push an inappropriate solution upon us; rather, they will refer us on to a specialist.

When selling, we should be the same. Our knowledge and professional manner should set us out as experts in our field. This will come across during our conversations with our customers. If our customer gains the impression that we know what we are talking about, and we are 'acting in their interest', we will elicit their trust. In this context, solutions that we offer will often be accepted; the same way as we are normally content to accept the solutions prescribed by our doctor.

This is not to be fatalistic. There are activities that need to be undertaken in order to achieve an amount of sales. Many of those activities, however, take place before we engage with a potential customer. If an ear, nose and throat specialist only sees patients with a stomach condition, with the best of intentions, they will never be able to help. If that specialist sees only two patients a year, they will never come to the aid of a satisfactory amount of people. Similarly, we must ensure our product or service is targeted properly. We must also build a pipeline of opportunities. We will only fulfil commercial objectives by targeting enough of the appropriate people. Once we do this, we can strive to improve our performance. There is an art to conveying possibility and solving problems and we can always try to be better.

PLANNING FOR THE FUTURE

Targets are not achieved by focusing on the transaction.

We have all experienced someone who inadvertently makes it apparent that they are putting the transaction first. We become victims of the sales person with '£' signs in their eyes and we do not trust them. We will not buy from that type of person unless we believe we have no alternative; which, in today's commercial environment, is unlikely. Even if we make a purchase, we will not enjoy the experience. It is unthinkable that we will either recommend them to others or return to them ourselves.

For a sales person to put themselves in this situation is not commercially viable. In a world that is so competitive we need to own the relationships with our customers. We need them to recommend us to others and we need them to make repeat purchases. Transactional selling makes this outcome less likely.

The opposite is also true. If we meet a sales person who only cares about the relationship; who we believe is 'acting in our interests' we will want to buy from that person and will keep going back. Because we feel that we can trust that person we will be willing to recommend them to family, friends and business contacts. If they cannot help and are honest enough to explain this; this will only solidify our trust in them. In this scenario, we are just as likely to recommend them to contacts as if we had used them ourselves.

Forgetting the transaction and concentrating on relationships allows us to build customers with a lifetime value. By always 'acting in our customers' interests' our relationship with them becomes like a partnership. We replace the time honoured adversarial relationship between supplier and customer wherein the two parties regard each other with extreme caution and the sales process feels more like a boxing match, rather than a conversation. Instead, we are working together to find a mutually beneficial solution.

Deconstructing the Myth of Benefit Selling

PART I: THE BUYER'S MOTIVATION

Two fundamental human motivations are:

- Pleasure; to gain reward.
- Pain; to avoid loss.

So many of the actions that we take in our lives can be attributed to these factors. This is certainly the case when examining our buying habits. We go out to eat, where the primary motivation may be to gain reward; and we buy insurance in order to avoid loss. On occasion, the two stimuli apply separately but often they apply together.

There are some activities in which we partake that can be explained by the motivation of gaining reward, such as going to a pop concert; a friend's party; or indulging in our favourite ice cream on holiday. This does not have to be the case though, as any of these activities could also be undertaken to avoid loss. For example, we may go to the pop concert for pleasure or we may only go because our friends will be there. The motivation for attending is then one of not missing out; which is loss avoidance. Similarly, the ice cream, may be eaten purely for pleasure or because we are feeling sorry for ourselves. In the latter case, once again, the motivation becomes avoidance of loss. It is, of course, quite possible for both motivations to be working together in any of these examples.

OUR PRIMARY MOTIVATION

It is widely acknowledged, in the world of psychology, that the avoidance of loss is a more powerful motivator than that of gaining reward. For example:

These days there is not much we would be prepared to give up in order to earn an extra £10; for most of us, it is not a vast sum of money. However, what happens if you put your hand in your pocket and realize you are missing £10? Most of us will look around where we are sitting, lifting the cushions off the sofa. We will retrace our steps, look in our cars and may even ask others if they have seen it; often, in a somewhat accusatory tone.

The point is; we will spend a lot more energy looking for, and worrying about, the £10 that we lost than we would ever put in to earning £10. Even several days after the loss, it may still be niggling away, somewhere at the back of our minds.

The primacy that the avoidance of loss has, over gaining reward, can be seen in all aspects of our lives:

Many of us will happily contribute to worthy causes such as a breast cancer charity. However, the biggest contributors will tend to be those who have lost friends and family members to the disease. Not wishing to experience this type of loss again, these people are more motivated to do something about it.

There is no better example to illustrate the central part that 'the avoidance of loss' has on us than in the world of work. Most people would happily admit that if they were to win the lottery they would quit their jobs. Even those of us who would not quit would have all sorts of caveats: we may decide not to work on Mondays or Fridays and we could all probably think of at least one or two clients with whom we would no longer wish to deal!

The point is that the majority of people do not go to work to gain reward. If this were the case, winning the lottery would make no difference. Having £10 million in the bank would not negate the salary we earn at work; we would still receive it. The reality is that our motivation for going to work is the avoidance of loss. If we do not work, we cannot run our cars, we cannot pay the mortgage, we cannot feed the family and we cannot go on holiday. However, if we were to win the lottery and had £10 million in our bank account, we would be able to do all those things; so our salary would not matter any more.

This is an important point for, if most of us go to work to avoid loss, then companies, by definition, are full of people who are risk averse. Why is it then, that when people are selling, they use benefits; which are about gaining reward? Taking this approach means there is a complete mismatch between the way people are selling and the way people buy. It is completely illogical.

In business, a person's primary motive for buying new software will not be to become more efficient. They will buy the software in order to avoid wasting money, miss opportunities or lose market share to their competitors. If one's competitors are becoming more efficient, then we also have to remain efficient in order to stay in the race. It is all avoidance of loss. People in business rarely buy to gain reward. Almost everyone in business is 'risk averse':

We have all had customers with whom we have had really positive negotiations and they have told us they want to go ahead with the order. Weeks and months then go by, during which time they offer numerous excuses for not being able to confirm. Six months later, you get a call to say not only do they now want to go ahead, but they need it yesterday! This is because they waited until the absolute last minute, when they had no choice other than to place the order. This is classic behaviour of people buying to avoid loss.

Rarely will someone place an order with you and ask you to deliver any time in the next six months. This is not how businesses work. When someone does, it is normally because they must spend their budget in order not to lose it the following year. You, as the supplier, may get an order early, but their motivation is still avoidance of loss. Businesses do not spend money unless they think they must. Everything they do is to avoid loss, not to gain reward. They will either keep their cash until they can manage no longer or they will not spend it at all.

It is not just in business that our motivation is avoidance of loss. In life generally, the avoidance of loss is normally a greater motivator than gaining reward.

Most of us spend the majority of our waking lives at work because if we do not, we cannot pay the mortgage and feed the family. We pay the mortgage because otherwise we will not have a roof over our head; so many of our practical everyday purchases are of this type. We put petrol in our car, otherwise it will not run. We buy milk and bread, otherwise we cannot have breakfast. Even the discretionary and lifestyle purchases that we make have avoidance of loss as a major factor. We will buy items to keep up with our friends or so as not to miss out on the latest fashions or trends. We will often buy major brands in order to maintain the status and reputation that we have, or to make us feel better about ourselves.

If, with a little reflection, we realize that most people, most of the time, do things to avoid loss, why do we cling to the myth that we should sell benefits, which are all about gaining reward?

PART II: BENEFITS DON'T WORK

Benefit selling is an approach borne out of the transactional model.

Benefit selling is all about the sales person; it is not about the customer.

WHOSE BENEFITS ARE THEY?

Sales people, who are trained in this method of selling, naturally think in terms of 'their' benefits. Marketing departments will produce literature, espousing the supposed benefits 'they' have to offer. The danger of this approach is that it is not customer focused. This is because there is a disparity between the language of the sales person and the marketing department, and the way customers buy.

People's primary motivation, most of the time, is the avoidance of loss and, therefore, their principle concerns are rarely the benefits. For example, businesses do not buy to be more profitable; they are more concerned with not wasting money and missing opportunities. So, one could say to a business owner:

> 'This software will allow you to streamline your finance department and, therefore, be more profitable.'

Alternatively one could say:

> *'This software will allow you to streamline you finance department and, therefore, not waste money on unnecessary processes and personnel.'*

Needless to say, because the second example taps in directly to the business owner's primary motivation for the purchase, it is more powerful.

Working with benefits in mind cannot result in a customer-focused approach because you are not thinking like your customer. Using benefits forces you to work in a language which buyers do not use.

Whether people are buying to avoid loss or gain reward, they always buy to solve problems.

Thinking in terms of benefits does not align you with this reality. This means you can end up working in a theoretical arena which bears little or no relation to your customer, because you never understand the primary motivations for the purchase. So, even if we were to assume that people go out to eat solely to gain reward; benefits will still miss the point. For example:

'La Caseta', is a little Italian restaurant. It is the best restaurant in town but also the most expensive. Because of this, many people only go there for special occasions. The benefits of the restaurant are clear:

- It has the best food, which means you will have the most delicious meal.
- It has the best service, catering for your every whim; which means you are always made to feel special.
- It has the best atmosphere, which means you always have a great time.

A restaurant, in this position, may market themselves **solely** on these benefits. However, none of these, in its own right, provides the initial motivation for the customer to visit that restaurant. The underlying problem that this restaurant solves for its patrons, who cannot afford to dine there very often, is:

- Where can I go to mark a special occasion?
- Where can I go that will show a loved one that I care?
- Where can I go that is worthy of what I have to celebrate?

The benefits simply become solutions to the problem.

The primary motive for buying will not be; **'We have the best food in town.'**

The motivator is more likely to be; **'How do you show a loved one that you care?'**

The solution then, is by giving them 'the best food and service in a wonderful setting'. It is by thinking in terms of problems that you **really** start to understand your customer's motivations. The risk of thinking in terms of benefits is that you never truly understand the primary motive behind your customer's purchase.

Marketing departments, as well as sales people, are making mistakes like this every single day. Thinking in terms of benefits means marketing departments can produce material that is ineffective. For sales people, it will result in missed opportunities.

By buying into this misnomer, we start to employ another term so often used by sales and marketing departments which is equally unhelpful. Once we start using the term 'benefits' we also slip into the idea of 'needs'. In the same way that 'benefits' force us to think in a way contrary to our customers, 'needs' do the same.

Henry Ford said: 'If I had asked my customers what they wanted, they'd have said a faster horse.' The problem with the idea of 'needs' is that they presuppose that the customer knows what they want. Customers who are unaware of the array of possibilities available to them will not know what they want. Moreover, some customers will not even be aware that they have a problem.

As the sales person, you are the expert and you are the educator. It is your mission to explore avenues with your customers. If you pre-suppose that they know what they want, they may make a wrong purchase and blame you. Words like 'benefits' and 'needs' are not only inappropriate; they are completely irrelevant. The only way to be effective in selling or marketing is to think the same way as your buyer. Benefit selling does not allow you to do this, but people have been indoctrinated with the idea of benefit selling for so long, they believe it and are left struggling.

PLATITUDES

> 'the quality or state of being dull or insipid. A banal, trite, or stale remark' (Merriam-Webster)

> 'a remark or statement that has been used too often to be interesting or thoughtful' (English Oxford Dictionary)

Without developing a relationship with our customer, any promises we make will sound like platitudes. As buyers, we have heard them all before. To be told something is the cheapest, the best, the most efficient, the most reliable or the safest, etc., has almost no impact anymore. Moreover, it is almost impossible for a sales person to develop a good relationship with a customer based on benefits. Benefits are always, by their very nature, the destination. They are 'the promised land'. They are not the reality that the customer is facing. Initially, the only effective way to engage with a customer is to base the conversation on their reality; that is, where they are today. It is not credible to start a conversation based on where you think you can take them.

As attractive as it is, 'the promised land' is always a scary, faraway place. It may be desirable, but it is still daunting. If it were that easy to get to, the customer would already be there. Moreover, the journey itself may present difficulties. If a sales person talks about the destination without addressing the difficulties of the journey, they are liable to miss concerns which their customer harbours. Their solution will be incomplete and they will rightly fail to secure any business.

By using benefits, there is also a danger of mis-selling or overselling. Companies and sales people try to 'out benefit' each other to the point that they inadvertently create unrealistic expectations in the eyes of their customer. This is one of the reasons why many of us have felt let down by a purchase we have made. While trying to 'out benefit' competitors, sales people will often find they reach a glass ceiling and have nothing else to offer. The end result of this 'benefits approach' is that products and services often lose their differentiation and become commoditized.

CREATING OBJECTIONS

If someone offers me benefits, and they do not know me very well, they sound like platitudes. Then what happens?

Not only are we sophisticated buyers, but we are also cynical. This is because we are bombarded with so many marketing messages, making promises, all the time. We have also all been let down by a purchase we have made. So, while a sales person is giving us the 'benefits', our natural state of mind is one where we look for the catch. Benefit selling does not compel the sales person to match the benefits to their customer's reality. Instead, benefits are often the equivalent of just talking about the 'promised land'. The result is, it all sounds too good to be true.

Once a customer, mentally, is looking for the catch, the objections start flooding out. Benefit selling, by its very nature, creates objections and puts the customer in a defensive state of mind. The sales process then starts to become adversarial. It almost mimics a boxing match. While the sales person punches their customer into submission with benefits, the customer hits back with objections. This is not two people working together to come up with a solution; it is two people on opposite sides of the fence, jousting.

Benefit selling and platitudes will always create objections. Not only do they create a barrier between the sales person and the customer, but benefits do not force you to get into the mindset of your customer. In fact they often lead to the opposite. Even if a customer is not looking for the catch, without a proper understanding of their buying motivations and by focusing on the benefits, a sales person can make comments that lose a sale, even when they have the right product. For example:

A direct marketing company helps drive business by introducing its customers to potential clients. A sales person from the marketing company has a meeting with a potential customer. Their main motivation for attending is to see if they can even out the peaks and troughs of their sales cycle. The sales person talks about all the benefits of using their company and how they deliver new business. This marketing company could help. However, the sales person never directly addresses the potential customer's main motivation. This leaves them in doubt that the sales person truly understands their predicament.

Moreover, by talking up the amount of business they can create, the sales person inadvertently introduces an objection. Their potential customer is only looking for a certain level of business at particular times of the year. During the meeting they become concerned that they will not be able to cope, although they do not want to admit this to the sales representative. Inevitably, no sale takes place, even though the marketing company had a solution which would have worked.

MAKING EVERYTHING IDENTICAL

Benefit selling will also make your product or service sound the same as everyone else's. This is because, in whatever area we are making a purchase, there are only ever a few benefits that we are seeking. So, for example, in business we may want to achieve a healthy work/life balance, run the business more efficiently, more profitably and stay ahead of the competition. After that, there really are not that many benefits that matter. So when companies drill down their message to these core benefits, every business becomes identical.

You have a morning meeting with a recruitment company. The essence of their 'presentation' is that you should be using them for your staff recruitment and they give you the following 'benefits':

1   We will do all the leg work for you; which means you will save a lot of time and we will give you a better work/life balance.
2   Instead of you sifting through CVs during your working day, we will do that for you so you can concentrate on running the company; which means that you will be more efficient.
3   We have a wide candidate pool and are more likely to find the right candidates and fill that vacant position faster, which means less staff overtime to cover; which in turn also means you will be more profitable.
4   Our candidates bring a wealth of experience and ideas from similar industries and are more likely to work out and stay with you longer; making you more competitive.

They leave your office and seem to have made a compelling argument. The benefit of commissioning them is that they will:

1   Give you a better work/life balance.
2   Make you more efficient.
3   Make you more profitable.
4   Make you more competitive.

What a great recruitment firm!

The same afternoon, an IT company has a meeting with you. The essence of their 'presentation' is that you should be using them for your IT requirements and they give you the following 'benefits':

1   We will be proactively managing your IT system so it rarely goes down, relieving you of having to stay late in the office to sort out software problems; which means you will save a lot of time and we will give you a better work/life balance.
2   Instead of you fighting viruses that have slowed your system down and checking e-mails to eradicate spam, we will do that for you so you can concentrate on running the company. You will be able to work faster and harder; which means that you will be more efficient.
3   We remotely monitor your computer management system 24/7 which will enable you to drastically reduce your administrative downtime and work smarter; which means you will be more profitable.
4   Our IT people bring a wealth of experience from other industries and are able to advise you on the latest software so you can stay one step ahead of your competition; which means you will be more competitive.

They leave your office and they also seem to have made a compelling argument. The benefit of commissioning them is that they will:

1   Give you a better work/life balance.
2   Make you more efficient.
3   Make you more profitable.
4   Make you more competitive.

Haven't you heard that somewhere else today?

Any system of selling that can make a recruitment firm and an IT firm sound the same is ridiculous. In a world where we are all striving to stand out from the crowd, benefit selling achieves exactly the opposite.

Using this method, you do not just sound like your competitors; you sound like everybody.

The myth of benefit selling has persisted for far too long. **For your customers, there are no benefits, just problems and solutions.** Let us hope that once and for all, this legend has finally been laid to rest.

Stop Using Benefits – Start Using Problem Maps™

5

In order to help us understand our customers, we need to recognize the problems that we solve for them. Every purchase solves a problem. Therefore, by working in terms of problems that we solve, rather than benefits that we provide, we will achieve clarity in our sales messages. It is only by defining our products or services in terms of problems solved, that we ensure we stay completely customer focused. This is because, by taking this approach, we are always working in terms of what motivates our buyer.

Because every consumer or business has a finite amount of resources available to them, they will prioritize their purchasing. Some purchases will happen regularly; for example, food or stationery. Other purchases may be rare, for example, buying a car or house. How quickly we deal with problems will often be determined by the risk involved in the purchase. In the main, the greater the perceived risk, the longer the sales cycle. This is for two main reasons:

1   If we perceive the risk to be big, then we are more concerned not to make a mistake. So, we may only buy a sofa, for our living room, a few times in our lives and it is a significant item in terms of our resources. Therefore, because we will have to live with any decision we make for a long time, we will take a lot of care to avoid making the wrong one.

2   The bigger the risk and the bigger the decision, the more people are likely to be involved in the process. Most of us will happily purchase a chocolate bar without asking anyone else because the ramifications of the purchase are so small. However, if a business is purchasing new software, it may impact on a variety of different people and departments. There may be a significant outlay in purchasing the software and in training the staff how to use it. There may also be an impact on the way in which people work. Therefore, many people may be involved in the decision.

Similarly, if a couple are moving house, it is likely that they will reach a decision together. Moreover, they may ask trusted friends or family to also be involved and give them advice.

The more people involved in a decision, the longer it takes. This is because logistically, it takes time to involve everyone and a consensus often has to be reached. In fact, because we are all more motivated by the avoidance of loss rather than gaining reward most of the time, we will rarely take action on a problem until we feel we are left with no other choice. So, the company will not buy the software until the cost and issues presented by not buying it are greater than those if they do make the purchase. Similarly, people will put off moving house and only do so when the consequences of not moving are more severe than making the move.

Ultimately, people make purchases to solve problems. Either the problem starts small and grows until action needs to be taken, or the wherewithal is found, so action can be taken. Alternatively, problems can appear and action can be taken immediately. For example, if your roof starts leaking water into your house, you are likely to call someone to fix it straight away. Sometimes the risk in solving the problem may be so small, or the resource needed so little, that taking immediate action has no long term ramifications. For example:

1   Jim enters a supermarket to do the weekly shop. On display are some beautiful pineapples. The point of sale display conveys

possibility to Jim. He was unaware these pineapples were available. Jim adores pineapple and they look and smell delicious. His problem immediately becomes one of not wanting to miss out. The purchase is so small that he takes immediate action and purchases a pineapple as part of his weekly shop.

2   Sarah and Jim drive a small car and are expecting their first child. They are aware they will have a problem when the baby arrives, because there will be insufficient room to fit all the baby equipment in their current vehicle. At the time, they do not feel they have the funds to purchase a new car but they do start to work this purchase into their future plans. Moreover, the problem is only small, as the baby is not yet born.

3   When the baby arrives, Sarah and Jim often find themselves struggling with the weekly shop, the baby, the buggy, etc. As this problem develops, Sarah and Jim recognize they cannot put off replacing the car any longer. When they do start looking to buy a new car, they spend quite a while surfing the Internet, reading magazines, asking friends and visiting showrooms. For them, the purchase is fairly high risk as they will keep this car for a long time and it will be expensive. They will also have to agree on the car together, and therefore it will be a compromise between their different priorities.

PROBLEMS AND VALUE

In a low cost or low risk sale, a customer may only need to recognize one small problem in order to justify a purchase. Jim's only problem when purchasing his pineapple is one of missing out. However, in a high cost or high-risk sale, often a singular problem is not enough to justify the purchase in the customer's mind. It will be a few, combined problems, and the resulting issues caused by these, that start to make the purchase seem compelling.

For Sarah and Jim, the initial problem was that the car was too small. As a result of this, every journey becomes an ordeal and time consuming because they have to strategically work out how to fit everything in. It may mean that they cannot take everything they want with them. They may, therefore, suddenly realize their baby needs something they decided to leave behind. As a result, planned day trips become difficult as they often find themselves caught short and inconvenienced. They, therefore, rarely go on long journeys or visits. The initial problem may not have seemed big enough to justify the purchase of a new car; however, the issues that this initial problem causes start to make the purchase seem more worthwhile. In time, Sarah and Jim will come to this realization on their own, and will probably make the purchase.

If they had visited a car showroom to look at what was available before their child was born, they would not have yet had this realization and probably would not have bought the car. However, a sales person who understood the problem of having a small car and the issues resulting from travelling with a new baby could have altered their awareness of the situation. That sales person, by developing the problems, would show Sarah and Jim there was more value in an earlier purchase than they realized. By conveying possibility and solving problems, the sales person may have made a sale that others would not have.

Over the course of time, Sarah and Jim will buy a new car anyway, but perhaps they would not have had to go through the heartache they experienced before they made the purchase.

In order for sales people to understand where they add value, it is not enough to know the problems that they solve. They must also understand the issues that will be caused by those problems. It is only then that one can see the value one adds and to whom.

DEVELOPING THE CONVERSATION

It is impossible to develop a good relationship with a customer based around benefits. They will just sound like platitudes and empty promises. It is much easier to develop the conversation and relationship based around problems; for you are engaging a customer around their present reality. You are inevitably talking about their issues and their concerns. You will also be adding value if you introduce ideas they have not thought of previously. You are not starting a conversation based on the solutions (the promised land – their destination) but based around problems which they can easily understand (their current situation).

You do not pick up a plane from London to New York in New York; you pick it up in London and it then takes you to New York. Equally, it is only logical that you do not start your conversation at your destination; (which benefit selling does). You start at where your customer is today (their initial buying motivations – problems) and then together go on your journey.

If a sales person only understands the obvious problems they solve, they will not be able to develop a sale. The conversation will be very one-dimensional, as will the questions the sales person asks. Moreover, as obvious problems are often self-evident, it is also less likely that the sales person will add any value to their customer by exploring areas the customer had not previously considered. It is only when a sales person has a deeper understanding of not just the obvious problems, but the issues these may cause, that an interesting and valuable conversation can ensue.

INTRODUCING PROBLEM MAPS™

Problem Maps™ are literally a way of mapping the problems and issues your product or service solves. In order to achieve clarity in our sales message, we need to understand the problems that we solve and the issues caused by those problems. With this understanding it becomes easier to:

1 **Recognize whether our product or service is commercially viable.** This is done by immediately being able to see the array of problems we solve. From this, it is easy to consider whether these problems are compelling, and to whom, and whether we can sell the solution at a price it is worth the customer paying.

2   **Produce engaging marketing material.** A Problem Map™ shows us our buyer's motivations. We can, therefore, produce material based on these.
3   **Have meaningful conversations with customers.** Because we will have a proper understanding of where we add value we will know the areas we should discuss with our customer to ascertain whether we have a solution for them.

So, the Problem Map™ is a mechanism to enable you to understand the problems you solve and the issues those problems cause. It encourages a person to think about buyer motivations. It enables someone to quickly and easily understand the plethora of areas their product or service covers and where they can really add value. From this, they can really get clarity into their sales messages. It is not something to be undertaken one time only, but an exercise that needs to be repeated on a consistent basis. How often one produces a new Problem Map™ will depend on the speed at which your particular market place evolves. Sales people who are regularly talking to customers will be the first to recognize new problems emerging. Equally, a problem that may have been a compelling reason to buy a few months ago may, over time, become irrelevant. For this reason Problem Maps™ will often need updating.

CREATING A PROBLEM MAP™

If possible, it is easier to create a Problem Map™ with a few people than to try and do it on your own. The Problem Map™, in many ways, is like a brainstorming session. In an ideal world, the Problem Map™ will be backed up by speaking with existing customers and market research. Of course, those people within a company who regularly talk to their customers may be able to produce an excellent Problem Map™ based on the customer experience they already have.

To produce a Problem Map™, it is best to use an A1 size sheet of paper or a large white board. If you are using A1 paper, turn it horizontally. Along the top should be four different headline problems that you can solve for your customer. Each one of these headline problems **must** be different from the others. Underneath each headline problem, should be three issues that the headline problem will cause. Although the three issues under each headline problem should be different from one another, it is fine for them to overlap with issues in another column. A particular issue that keeps appearing would indicate itself to be important. The result of this exercise is a map with a maximum of 16 problems on it. One would normally expect some overlap between the issues in the different columns and therefore, it is unlikely there will be 16 unique problems. For example, Table 5.1 features 14 unique problems.

	Headline problem 1	Headline problem 2	Headline problem 3	Headline problem 4
Headline problem	I am looking for a suitable candidate and cannot find anybody.	I am too busy to undertake the whole recruitment process.	I will never be able to draw candidates for the whole market on my own.	I need someone now and can't wait to undertake the process, e.g. advertise, etc.
Resulting problem 1	Morale in the office reduces as other staff are overworked.	Business suffers as I am trying to undertake too many activities.	It takes much longer to find someone than it should.	I may lose customers who I let down.
Resulting problem 2	I start to lose customers who I let down as we are under-resourced	Opportunity/cost. It is costing a fortune undertaking recruitment instead of billing for client time.	I may not recruit the best person available for the position (maybe competitors will get this person).	Home life suffers as I am having to do two jobs
Resulting problem 3	Margins are hit as we have to pay staff increased overtime.	Home life suffers as I have to spend more time in the office to get everything done.	High attrition rate as I compromise on candidates and ultimately recruit the wrong people.	Loss of reputation as we can't deliver on our promises

Table 5.1: An example of a Problem Map™ for an imaginary recruitment company, Fictional Recruitment.

Our Problem Map™ helps the employees at Fictional Recruitment start to understand where they add value. Fictional Recruitment charge 20% of the first year's salary as their fee. A potential customer recruiting a £30,000 position may not see £6000 worth of value in the headline problems alone. However, as we start to see the results that the headline problems cause, £6000 no longer seems a large amount. Losing reputation, customers or putting significant pressure on someone's home life can all make the £6000 seem like a good investment.

Table 5.1 is a typical Problem Map™. One can see that the headline problems are all different, as are the three resulting problems within each individual vertical column. However, it is fine for resulting problems to appear in more than one column. We can see the loss of customers and the strain on one's home life appear on more than one occasion.

With the understanding the Problem Map™ gives, it will be much easier to engage with a customer. Using the Problem Map™, the sales person will not have a trite conversation based around their service, but will be able to explore areas that are likely to be of concern to their customer. These of course, will be the areas where they can really add value.

When working on a Problem Map™, you must not just limit yourself to practical problems. For example, if you are preparing a Problem Map™ for a luxury dress shop, some of your problems will be emotional. You may be helping people solve problems to do with status and aspirations. Some retailers may also be solving an activity displacement problem. Depending on the business, you must be willing to explore the emotional problems you solve. After all, there are brands that almost exclusively solve emotional problems. Think of luxury watch or car brands. These days you do not need an expensive brand name on a watch for it to keep good time or on a car for it to drive well. However, this would be missing the point. The luxury brands solve emotional problems which others cannot.

Undertaking only one Problem Map™ may not be sufficient. You will need to have a separate Problem Map™ for the different situations in which your potential customers may find themselves. Table 5.1 for Fictional Recruitment is a map for those potential customers who do not currently have a recruitment supplier and are undertaking the process themselves. However, Fictional Recruitment may also want to market and sell their services to those companies that already have a supplier of recruitment services. They would therefore have to create a separate Problem Map™ based on the issues potential clients might have with their current supplier. Similarly, many companies do not sell solely to end users, while some companies do not deal with the end user at all. These companies would require a Problem Map™ looking at the issues that third party introducers or distributors may have. Ultimately the number of Problem Maps™ required will depend on the variety of different audiences to whom you market and sell.

	Headline problem 1	Headline problem 2	Headline problem 3	Headline problem 4
Headline problem	**Not seeing the amount of candidates I expected.**	**I am being supplied with too many inappropriate candidates.**	**The whole process is taking too long.**	**I am happy with the service but the business is at risk as I am overly reliant on this one supplier.**
Resulting problem 1	It is taking too long to find the right person.	Costing me money as I am wasting my time in pointless interviews.	Margins are being hit as we have to pay more staff overtime.	If they were to let me down, it would have an adverse affect on my own customers.
Resulting problem 2	My attrition rate is higher than it should be because I am compromising on who I hire.	Home life is affected as I am spending more time interviewing than I should be and therefore struggling to get everything done.	Staff morale is low because they have to work increased hours to cover.	I would be completely reliant on staff overtime which would severely damage margins.
Resulting problem 3	Service delivery suffers as I am not getting the best people for the job.	Business is suffering as I spend more time on recruitment than I should be.	We are letting customers down as we are working at full stretch for longer than we anticipated.	The business would suffer as I would have to fire fight this problem taking me away from other activities.

Table 5.2: A second example of a Problem Map™ produced by our imaginary company, Fictional Recruitment, for potential customers who already have a supplier.

SO, WHY NOT 'BENEFIT MAPS'?

It would not be unreasonable if one has been trained to think in terms of benefits to decide to do a benefit map. However, this would be less than helpful. Every purchase solves a problem. The purpose, therefore, is to understand the motivations of the buyer when purchasing a product or service. Benefits, on their own are meaningless. They are just an advantage that your product or service has which is completely irrelevant to the buyer. They will only become relevant if they solve a problem. At that point, they are no longer a benefit; they are a solution.

Because benefits are not about buyer motivations, working in benefits becomes generic and unhelpful. For example, imagine undertaking a Problem Map™ for two different types of restaurant:

Quickie Burger is a fast food hamburger restaurant. Among the problems it solves are:

- Needing food on the run.
- Needing a cheap meal out.
- Needing activity displacement for the children.

La Caseta is a posh, expensive restaurant. Among the problems it solves are:

- Needing to mark a special occasion.
- Needing to impress a client or potential partner.
- Needing activity displacement for adults.

People will have different motivations for visiting these two very different establishments. Therefore, the Problem Map™, for each one, is likely to be very different. Although some of the benefits of visiting either establishment will vary, it is completely possible that they will make many of the same claims. For example:

- Both may claim the benefit of using good quality produce, resulting in good food.
- Both may claim to have a good atmosphere.
- Both may claim good customer service.

A benefit map, if there were such a thing, would be much less stark in its differences than its equivalent Problem Map™. Any system of selling which presents these two, very different, establishments in similar terms is at best unhelpful and at worst complete nonsense.

Only by looking at problems will you get to the heart of buyer motivation; therefore, only by looking at problems can anyone really start to understand the value that they give and to whom.

UNDERSTANDING IMPLICIT AND EXPLICIT PROBLEMS

There is one piece of the jigsaw that is still missing when talking in terms of problems. Without this understanding, your problem selling could literally be a disaster.

In 1959 there was a famous cigarette commercial in the UK for 'Strand' cigarettes. Its notoriety is attributed to the fact that it is hailed as one of the least successful TV commercials ever made. The commercial featured a Frank Sinatra lookalike, lighting up a cigarette in an empty street with a romantic backing track and the strap line reading; 'You're never alone with a Strand' Now how romantic is that?

What happened?

The public loved it! Due to public demand, the backing track; titled 'The lonely man theme' was released as a single and went to 39 in the UK charts. Likewise, the Sinatra lookalike went on to become a well-known British actor.

So what went wrong?

Smoking in the 1950s was a very social habit; something you did amongst friends and colleagues. As a result of the commercial, the public associated Strand cigarettes with being lonely. Sales of the brand bombed and it was soon withdrawn from the market.

THE DEODORANT EFFECT

In order to understand what went wrong with the Strand cigarette campaign, we need to introduce an idea that I call 'the deodorant effect'.

If you have taken the essence of Problem Maps™ on board and you are selling a male deodorant, it would be reasonable to assume that one of the problems your deodorant solves is that it prevents men, who have a personal hygiene issue, from smelling. If you take the instructions on creating Problem Maps™ too literally, you could be excused for commissioning an advertising campaign with headlines such as: 'Do you smell?' or 'Do you find that no one wants to go near you?'

This is perhaps an even worse copy line for an advertisement than the Strand cigarette example. The reason for its failure, however, is going to be the same as that of Strand cigarettes. By being too explicit about a problem, your product or service is at risk of becoming associated with the problem, rather than the solution. So, if a deodorant brand were to advertise publicly in the terms described above, the implication would be; anyone buying that deodorant smells and no one wants to go near them. Therefore, no one would want to buy the deodorant, because purchasing it would indicate one is suffering from those issues.

Deodorant companies do not make this mistake. What they often do is imply the problem in some way, without being too explicit.

For example, an unexciting man may walk down the street without drawing too much attention to himself. With one spray of the deodorant, he suddenly receives the welcome advances of attractive looking women. The problem of not being able to attract the opposite sex is not explicitly mentioned in any way. In fact the opposite is true. This deodorant is now associated with success when it comes to attracting the opposite sex. The problem, however, is implied within the advertisement and, therefore, touches the real buying motivations of a potential customer.

Some commercials will do the opposite. They will directly show the problem but in such a severe and far-fetched way that it is implausible that anybody can suffer from it to that extent. While this can be potentially more dangerous, if executed well, the same effect is achieved. That is, the problem is implied without incriminating the potential purchaser.

So, in a private communication with a customer, a sales person may be able to be more explicit about the issues. This will be especially true as the relationship develops. However, one still needs to be careful. In a one-to-one dialogue, therefore, examples of other people or companies that have previously been helped can be very useful. It allows a sales person to talk about the problem without explicitly implying that the customer they are facing is suffering from it. As being too direct can sometimes feel accusatory or threatening, this can be a very effective tool.

When the communication is public, such as advertising or point of sale material, it will be very unlikely that the problem should be mentioned in an explicit way, for then you will have to solve a problem that people do not mind publicly admitting they have. While there may be examples of this, they are few and far between. Once your sales message is in the public domain, the normal rule of thumb will be to imply the problem without making it too explicit. This will often involve showing a success (a solution to the problem) but not showing the problem itself, as in our deodorant example. This is not, however, benefit selling because:

- The success has to be related directly to a problem we can help solve.
- The problem, however understated, should be implied. In some very successful consumer advertising, this can be very subtle, but it is there.

Problem Maps™ are the best way of obtaining clarity in your sales messages. How the information obtained is then executed should depend on the environment in which one is working. Careful thought must go into this process to ensure success.

Why the USP Stops you Selling

In 1961 Rosser Reeves, the Chairman of US advertising agency, Ted Bates & Company, articulated to the world the concept of the 'USP' in his book 'Reality in Advertising'. In it, he explained that the 'Unique Selling Proposition' was a benefit, unique to you, that will attract new customers.

Since then, it has been grossly misused. Over the years, many people have misinterpreted the USP to mean: why am I different? Of course this is not the same question. You could be the tallest insurance broker in the world. Whilst this would make you unique, it is not a benefit for your customers and is unlikely to be a reason why people would use your service. Just being different is not the same as having a USP.

The essence of the USP is important; that is, what is unique about my product or service that will attract new customers? The journey that you take in order to reach a conclusion is vital. The problem with the USP is that it channels your thinking in the wrong way. This prevents you from producing the most compelling offering available. Ultimately, it is the wrong question to be asking.

Any benefit, you can introduce, that is unique to you and that will attract new customers, is likely to be copied, and quickly. This is especially true today, as there are more businesses providing similar products and services than ever before. In this environment there will be other companies, similar to your own, able to clone your USP with ease.

Access to information also makes a difference. We live in such a fast-paced global market, where everything is on the Internet and where people can compare and contrast quickly and easily. Years ago, when the dissemination of information was not as quick or as easy, it may have taken longer for a USP to be copied. Today, this can happen almost instantly. Moreover, geographical boundaries meant that several companies could offer the same USP, but it would be unique to their individual audiences in their particular area. Today, so often, this is not the case. There are many products and services available where location is of no consequence and the Internet provides us with the wherewithal to source suppliers, not just nationally, but on a global basis.

ASKING A BETTER QUESTION

The Unique Selling Proposition makes us ask:

> *'What unique benefit can we promise that will attract new customers?'*

This is the wrong question.

The question we should be asking is:

> **'Why am I uniquely placed to solve the problem?'**

The difference between the questions

Every purchase solves a problem. Based on our Problem Map™, we know which problems we solve for our customers. Asking ourselves why we are uniquely placed to solve these problems keeps us thinking the same way as our buyers do and about their motivations, and will ensure that we stay aligned with their concerns. It forces us to ana-lyse ourselves, our product or service and the market place. In other words, we take a three-dimensional view. In so doing, it is more likely that we will create an offering that is original and has substance.

The Unique Selling Proposition, on the other hand, only asks us to think in terms of benefits. These do not address buying motivations. Thinking in terms of benefits does not force you to look at your prod-uct or service through your customer's eyes. It is, therefore, less likely that a company will come up with something truly compelling.

The danger of searching for a unique benefit that will attract new cus-tomers, is that it drives us to look at our product or service in a very one dimensional way. In Table 5.1 (page 55) and Table 5.2 (page 57), we put together two Problem Maps™ for a recruitment company. Being fic-tional, the maps are necessarily generic in nature and could therefore be applied to nearly all recruitment companies. Looking for a unique benefit we can offer to attract customers erroneously encourages us to focus on our product or service, rather than on our customer, and think in terms of what else we can offer. Even if we come up with something worthwhile, having taken a one-dimensional view, our idea is more likely to be superficial and therefore will be easier to copy. Then our uniqueness disappears once more. You can see this pattern happening in many market sectors as they become increasingly commoditized.

Therefore, it is preferable to ask our alternative question, 'Why am I uniquely placed to solve the problem?' It is perfectly possible, if we took a less generic example than Fictional Recruitment, that we would have a unique angle or idea. However, asking this question encour-ages us not to look at our product or service one-dimensionally. The question forces us to also think of our customer. We no longer attempt to just add more benefits to our recruitment service, but we start to look in other, possibly productive areas.

So, it may be that our previous background was accountancy. It may also be that as a two-man recruitment business, we can only really service companies within a 50 mile radius of our office. However, as native locals of the area, we can bring a real understanding of the region to our work. Therefore, 'Why am I uniquely placed to solve the problem?' forces us to develop our service in a way that adding benefits never would. By asking this question, Fictional Recruitment evolves from being a generic recruitment company to a financial recruitment company serving a particular region. This way we can bring our unique expertise of the industry, and of the area, to local companies that are struggling to find a suitable candidate in the financial sector.

We start to formulate a compelling case for why Fictional Recruitment is in a better position to solve this problem than anyone else. While in reality we would still need to develop Fictional Recruitment's proposition further, the principle is sound. The best way of producing a compelling proposition is by asking the question 'Why am I uniquely placed to solve the problem?'

Take John, a graphic designer, as another example. There is nothing unique about John. In fact, he is like every other graphic designer in town. Coming up with a USP in the traditional way is going to be extremely difficult. Even when he does, there will be no reason why it could not be used by one of his competitors. Asking the question; 'Why am I uniquely placed to solve the problem?' opens up other avenues. As well as graphic design, John has an interest in property and owns a couple of apartments which he rents out. It is likely he understands and knows more about property and property management than many other designers. John likes to meet his clients and works on his own. Therefore, it is sensible that he works within a 50 mile radius of his studio in North London.

John's graphic design business is now starting to evolve. He has experience in property and only wants to work within a 50 mile radius of North London. If you are a manufacturer in Scotland, John is not uniquely placed to solve the problem, but if you are a property company based in London, John may be. This is because he is local and can be at your beck and call. He also has an understanding of property as he deals in this sector himself.

Why would it make any difference at all if John deals in property or not?

Surely, graphic design is graphic design. Either you can do it, or you cannot.

This is true. However, a property company will employ a graphic designer to solve certain problems. They may need corporate literature in order to communicate better with their customers; they may need to stand out in the market place in order to create more awareness. Whatever their problem, they will perceive that a designer who understands property, even in a small way, is better placed to help. Imagine, as a property company, you are presented with two propositions:

- Graphic designer (*a*) (John): experienced, competent, nice guy, local, reasonably priced, some knowledge of the property market.
- Graphic designer (*b*): experienced, competent, nice guy, local, reasonably priced, but no property knowledge.

It is likely, in this scenario that the property company would use John. They would perceive he is in a better position to help them and solve their problem.

By asking yourself why you are uniquely placed to solve the problem, you start to mould your audience and your target market to your service and your skill sets. It may be that, in certain cases, you do have a uniqueness to your product or service that will attract new customers. However, solely exploring this area is too one-dimensional. You can become a compelling solution for some customers by looking at other areas.

Asking yourself, 'Why am I uniquely placed to solve the problem?' encourages you to put together a good sales strategy. If John, as a graphic designer, simply tried to sell his services to everybody he may succeed. However, by asking himself this question, he puts together a more compelling proposition and creates a niche market for himself. For companies working in property in London, he is now an obvious solution provider when they need graphic design. Of course, John must do a little research to ensure the market place is big enough to sustain his business. As a one-man business, however, it will not need to be very large to keep him busy.

As a small graphic design business, John does not have the budgets to undertake big advertising campaigns or extensive promotional programmes. Once John decides on a limited vertical market such as property, his strategy becomes clearer. For example, John can attend local property exhibitions and conferences. There may be an association with a local branch that he can join. John can also write articles for industry publications or relevant sections of a local paper. He may also want to advertise in these particular places. By asking 'Why am I uniquely placed to solve the problem?' John brings a focus to his business that makes it much more likely that he will succeed.

As a small business, John does not have the resources to build a brand or expertise in every sector across the country. He can, however, build a brand and expertise in certain areas of the market. Once John has a focus on property, as his business develops and expands, he may slowly widen the market place within which he works. For example, John may find that his business evolves into working with architects, surveyors and construction companies. Once an initial focus is successful, there will always be market opportunities to grow.

Your Emotional Selling Point and Giving Value

Creating a Problem Map™ starts to give us an understanding of where we add value. Every purchase solves a problem and the Problem Map™ allows us to identify the plethora of problems that we solve.

Asking: 'Why am I uniquely placed to solve the problem?' provides for the development of our product or service. The question encourages us to have a unique offering, or work with specific types of customer and market places, in order for our proposal to be compelling.

We start to give value when we appear to be in a good position to solve a particular customer's problem.

IS MY SOLUTION COST EFFECTIVE?

Of course, it should almost go without saying that your solution must be viable. If a customer's problem is costing them £500 per annum and you can solve it for £10,000, no one is going to use your solution. Unless there are some very severe consequences from this initial problem, it is just not worth spending £10,000 on its resolution.

If you have an energy saving solution for a private house which will reap the rewards over two or three years and you know that the average person stays in their house for ten years, the solution may be viable. If, however, it takes 20 years to get payback, it is clearly not a cost effective solution because very few people would remain in the same house long enough to realize their investment.

It is important to bear in mind that value comes not just from being able to solve a particular customer's problems but also doing it cost effectively. What is cost effective may, of course, depend on the affluence of your particular market place, for example, a luxury brand of car costing £150,000 may solve problems of status and aspirations, but only for extremely wealthy individuals.

VALUE AND RISK

Imagine you have a software package and you know that it can save an average company £5000 a year and, including training, the software costs £5000 to implement. Therefore, the company breaks even in the first year and thereafter saves £5000 per annum on its original costs. Even if a company only keeps the product for three or four years, they are going to be between £10,000 and £15,000 better off.

It seems clear that for the right company, there is value in this product. However, it is not that simple. The figures do not take into account the risk of the purchase. If the company employs 25 people, the business owner may reject your solution because of the risk and potential costs of that risk. For example:

- The staff may become less productive while they struggle to master the new package. This decrease in productivity may come at a significant cost to the company.

- Initially staff may make unnecessary mistakes as they come to terms with the new software. This may result in wrong deliveries and upset customers. Both could cost the company a lot of money.
- Implementing new software may mean attrition of staff who cannot come to terms with the new package.

In other words, although the apparent figures make the software appear great value, once the risks are considered, the likelihood of a positive payback looks less assured. Monetary value is therefore not as easy to measure as it first appears.

The more you can take the risk out of the decision, the easier it will be to make a sale. For example:

- Could you give the business owner testimonials from other satisfied customers where you have successfully installed the new software?
- Do you have case studies of where the software has been installed with little detriment to the business?
- Would it be possible to offer any sort of money back guarantee or refund of losses incurred should the software not work out?
- Is it worth offering a limited free trial in one particular department to prove how easy the software is to use?

Without being able to take some of the risk out of the transaction, you significantly reduce the value of the sale to your customer. We know that people are more motivated by avoidance of loss than gaining reward. Therefore, if your customer perceives the risk to be high, it is unlikely they will purchase.

Of course, this avoidance of loss does highlight another way of changing a customer's perception of risk. However hazardous a possible purchase may seem, if the risk of not purchasing appears even greater, then it still may be a gamble worth taking. So, if this particular business owner's competitors are all installing new software products, with all the potential efficiencies they can bring, then whatever the dangers of the purchase, it may be that the risk of being left behind is worse.

In order to understand value, it is not enough to analyse the monetary benefits of purchasing your product or service. One also has to be able to quantify the risk of both undertaking and not undertaking the purchase. Being able to minimize the risk will help tip the balance sheet and so make the purchase more desirable.

UNDERSTANDING EMOTIONAL VALUE

Emotional factors also need to be considered in every purchase. If your purchase solves mainly emotional problems then the emotional payback, rather than the monetary payback, is what matters. A person who buys a £10,000 watch is not concerned with the monetary value, but the emotional value it brings, for that person could buy a watch for £30 that would keep time accurately. The purchase solves problems such as status and aspirations. How effectively these problems are solved will determine whether a purchase is made.

This may seem obvious. However, even in practical purchases, emotional factors can determine the outcome. We have already highlighted the monetary value in our business owner's purchase of the software product and many of the practical risks they must take into consideration. Putting these aside, there will be emotional factors that will also affect the purchase. For example:

- People do not like change and find it emotionally unsettling. The business owner may be worried about any change the new software may bring.
- The software may also make the organization more IT dependent. If the business owner struggles with computers, they may not want to implement a solution that may find them wanting.
- There have been no requests of the business owner to look for a new software solution. By not implementing anything, no ques-

tions are likely to be asked in the foreseeable future. However, promoting new software will mean the business owner risking their own reputation.

Emotional agendas affect buying decisions even in business. They can prevent people buying, or be a major factor in a purchase:

> A new manager wanting to make their mark in a company may purchase a new product. While it may be advantageous to the business, the primary motive is to solve the problem of how to stamp their authority in their new position.

Moreover, one must remember that, even in business, one is still dealing with human beings who will have an emotional agenda that will encompass both personal and professional considerations. The two cannot be separated. Remember, for the most part, people go to work and lead a professional life to fund their personal existence.

For consumer and lifestyle purchases, emotional factors are usually the primary concern and more important than the practical and monetary considerations. Therefore, one must understand value is not a narrow concept. It is made up of both monetary and emotional factors, personal and professional agendas. One must also keep in mind the perceived risks the potential customer has in purchasing a particular product or service. It is only by taking all these things into consideration that one can start to ensure they deliver value, for enough customers, to make their solution commercially viable.

VALUE; THE BIGGER PICTURE

Sales Therapy® is an approach to selling that is relationship driven and not transactional. The old transactional model of selling encouraged us to sell and market **to** our customers. Companies would often engage in promotional activities which were there to 'interrupt' the consumer and make them pay attention. For example, if you were watching TV and the commercials came on, you tended to watch them. However, this interruption-based marketing is becoming less and less effective. Digital technology means we increasingly watch programmes on demand. We can flick through commercials on the radio and television with ease. Meanwhile, the sheer volume of direct mail and sales messages we receive means much of it goes unnoticed or forgotten. We also have access to spam filters and telephone and mailing list services, which allow us to prevent e-mails, letters and phone calls, if we wish.

The Internet has changed how we think. Today, customers are empowered with both choice and knowledge. We no longer want to passively be interrupted by marketing messages that are often irrelevant. Today, we like to participate. The most popular TV programmes are increasingly those that we do not just watch submissively, but get involved with. For example, *Big Brother* and *Pop Idol* allow us to vote on the outcome of the programme.

Sales and marketing is no longer something we do **to** customers, but **with** them. Nowadays we want to participate with brands, products and services. However, this will only be the case when customers perceive there is something in it for them. The only way to achieve this is to ensure your customer receives value from participating. Value is no longer something you only give a customer at the moment of purchase. If that is your approach, you may never reach that point. Moreover, if there is no ongoing value in the relationship, there will be no relationship. This may mean that opportunities to up-sell or for repeat business will go to a competitor. In many ways, whether we are delivering a product or service to our clients, we are primarily giving our customers an 'experience'. This means embarking on a journey with your customer, during which time, sales will be made.

Value can be given to a customer in many ways. When selling, you are a conveyer of possibility. In order to do this you need to be an expert in your field. Little nuggets of knowledge that keep customers informed, updated and provide insight will help you to develop a relationship. Your customer will deem it worthwhile to be associated with you. Moreover, delivering this knowledge will give you credibility and the customer will start to trust you.

There are many ways to put value into the relationship. It can be done by delivering free gifts or exclusive offers. Alternatively, one can make people feel special by giving them first access to a new product or service, or inviting them to an exclusive event.

Building up a network of contacts, who you can recommend to a customer when certain situations arise, is another way of adding value. You are no longer purely the provider of a particular product or service, but someone worth knowing who can help in a variety of unrelated situations.

You must be careful not to devalue what you do. For example, if you charge for your consultancy services by the hour, giving away an hour's free consultation may devalue your service. Why would anyone spend money on something they have had for free? In this scenario, providing a potential customer with a free paper you have written on a particular issue may be more helpful. It demonstrates your knowledge and expertise, whilst delivering something of value to your customer. You gain credibility and trust as it becomes evident that you are an expert in your field. It all points to making your consultancy services more attractive, rather than devaluing them. However you choose to deliver it, we can no longer just think of value as something that is given at the point of transaction. We also need to look at the bigger picture and that means delivering value throughout the relationship.

THE EMOTIONAL SELLING POINT (ESP)

Emotional considerations drive most consumer and lifestyle purchases. They also play an important part in business purchases. Therefore, we need to ensure that we deliver emotional value to our customer when they make a purchase. We do this through the Emotional Selling Point, or ESP. The ESP is the emotional problem that you solve for your customer and it is vitally important.

KEEPING COMPETITORS AT BAY

We have already discussed the dangers of a USP being copied, almost instantly, by a competitor. The ESP, however, is much harder to copy and, therefore, potentially more valuable. For example:

> Nike sell trainers. Trainers are a product that could easily become commoditized, for many of the trainers that we buy are manufactured in similar types of factory, in similar parts of the world. Nike is a premium brand, not just because of the product itself, but also because of the emotional value they give their customers. Nike stands for success and for winning and aim to dominate that emotion in the market place. When someone buys Nike trainers, they are not just buying a pair of shoes; they are buying a feeling and status with which they want to be identified. Anything with the Nike brand becomes more valuable because of the emotional value it gives; so T-shirts and caps displaying the Nike logo will sell at a premium price.

Having an Emotional Selling Point makes your product or service less vulnerable to the competition. It may be possible for another company to source almost exact replicas of the Nike range and to distribute them through similar outlets. Although the product itself may be similar, it will not be able to deliver the emotional value, and is therefore unlikely to threaten Nike's market share. Without an ESP, however, Nike becomes a commodity and therefore a company producing similar trainers, at a cheaper price, would possibly be able to challenge their position in the market place.

There are many examples of this. Harley Davidson stands for freedom and rebelliousness in a way that most other manufacturers do not. When people buy a Harley, they are not just buying a motorbike, but a lifestyle. Even those that do not own a bike will purchase T-shirts or other paraphernalia that have the logo emblazoned, in order to be associated with the emotional feelings the brand delivers.

USING THE ESP TO ENSURE CONSISTENCY

Creating an emotional attachment to your product or service and therefore giving your customer emotional value, makes it much harder for competitors to entice your customers away. The ESP, however, is not just for big companies and iconic brands; it is just as important for the small business owner. When they can, people buy products and services from companies they know and trust. This is because it is less risky making a purchase from these businesses.

In order for any business to build trust with their customers they have to be consistent. Trust comes from familiarity, and the reassurance that we know a company and what they deliver. If, every time we come into contact with a company, we receive a different message, we will never feel that we know them or understand them. Consequently it is unlikely that we will trust them, and, therefore, buy from them or recommend them to others.

It is for this reason that you have to be consistent throughout your company. This consistency will help the development of your brand. Whether it is a website, mailing piece, e-mail or phone call; every inter-action needs to deliver a consistent message. For many small busi-nesses, their people are the main way potential customers experience the brand, whether it is at a networking event, site visit or business meeting. How you dress and what hairstyle you have is often a major part of your customer's brand experience. If, as a business owner, you wear a suit one day, then jeans and a T-shirt the next; what message are you conveying? Inconsistencies will leave your potential customers confused. The result will be that they will not feel they can trust you.

Branding is all about the experience you give your customer and it does not start and end with a logo. It is what you wear, what you drive, the language you use, the business card you give out and everything else you do, say, and communicate in any number of ways. Your logo should not be blue because it is your favourite colour, but because it conveys your ESP.

Nike stands for winning and success. Harley Davidson stands for freedom and rebelliousness. If you are selling candles, you may stand for romance. A training company may choose to stand for empowerment. Charles Revson, founder of Revlon cosmetics famously said; 'In the factory we make cosmetics; in the drugstore we sell hope'.

Once you have decided on an appropriate ESP, you should benchmark everything you do against it. Your ESP is not something to be advertised for public consumption. Innately your customers should understand what you are about. Whether you stand for freedom, winning, hope, romance, empowerment or anything else; everything should be consistent with that emotion. Your business cards, website, e-mail, mailers and the way you dress and wear your hair should all deliver the same feeling. Not only will it be harder for competitors within your market to copy what you do and steal customers away, but this benchmarking will ensure consistency, which in turn will help to build trust.

If you get it right, the reassurance this will provide customers, will increase both sales and the recommendations you receive.

In order to understand what your ESP should be, you need to ask yourself:

- What emotional problems do I solve?
- What emotions do I want my customers to experience when they use my product or service?

For example, you may give hope to customers who are worried and, therefore, when they use your service, you may want them to feel relieved; or you may provide empowerment for people who feel vulnerable or scared and, therefore, you may want people who use your service to experience a new found confidence.

By brainstorming ideas to these questions, one will eventually identify an appropriate ESP.

Once you understand your ESP, you must ensure your company's message is always consistent. Moreover, as a business owner, your image should be consistent with the ESP, as well as that of your staff. Giving your customers value comes as a result of good strategic planning. Identifying and conveying your ESP and then benchmarking against it to ensure consistency is an important part of that plan.

Building Pipeline

8

Sales start by creating opportunities.

If you do not create opportunities then you are not going to get any sales. It is very similar to a football match. If you fail to create chances, you won't score any goals. You always have to be creating opportunities and, just as in a football match, you will often miss; when selling, there will be times when the sale will not materialize.

Successful selling starts with building pipeline. The whole sales process often goes wrong because people do not create enough opportunities. If you fail to ensure that you are always producing new opportunities, you will never have a robust sales process.

So many businesses find themselves hanging on to the bottom line for the one or two opportunities they have to come through. If they confirm both opportunities, they may hit their targets for that quarter. However, if one of the opportunities goes astray, suddenly the situation becomes critical. One then finds themselves desperate for the other deal to happen. Desperation can often lead to over-promising or, worse still, mis-selling.

In order to sell with integrity you have to be willing to walk away if you cannot help someone. It is easy to do this when you are in a position of strength. That means, ensuring you always have a solid pipeline of opportunities.

WHOSE RESPONSIBILITY IS PIPELINE?

Marketing departments have often been expected to generate leads to be followed up by sales people. Meanwhile, sales people have frequently been expected to create opportunities at the coal face, by knocking on doors and making cold calls. Today, the lines between sales and marketing have become ever more blurred. Purchases increasingly occur without direct human interaction. Traditional marketing tools such as promotional literature, which customarily were used to create awareness, will now, very often, combine with the Internet to take customers through a process that will lead to sales. Even when a consumer interacts with a sales person, they will often have undertaken their own research and will have already reached their purchasing decision. Literature found online and elsewhere, therefore, has to do the marketing and selling at the same time.

Take a company such as Amazon.com, the book e-retailer. Advertising, word of mouth and web marketing will encourage people to visit the site. The website itself is both a promotional tool and a sales tool in one; for example, the website will remember you, refer to your previous purchases and then recommend books which may be of interest. Amazon uses marketing tools to convey possibility to its users and will then have special offers to help drive sales. The entire website is one package. The shift from marketing to selling is seamless.

Every business must have a person or department that takes primary responsibility for sales and marketing as the two are indivisible. It may be a business owner who takes this role upon themselves, or it may be delegated to others. One of their primary objectives must be to ensure that a steady stream of opportunities is consistently created.

However, although building pipeline will be the responsibility of sales and marketing, it is something in which the whole company should be involved, for today's successful businesses need to be completely customer focused. Selling is about conveying possibility and solving problems. Ultimately, this means helping people and delivering value; putting the customer first. A customer focused and sales focused approach, therefore, are one and the same. The line where selling stops and good customer service begins is seamless. Today, successful companies must be both customer focused and sales-centric organizations. In a well-run business, everyone, to a greater or lesser extent, can be an income generator.

If your firm is an accountancy practice, you work for a sales organization first and then as an accountant. It does not matter how good an accountant you are: without sales you have no customers. Every company, therefore, is a sales organization and every employee who has contact with a customer, from the delivery driver to the business owner, will have an influence on them and whether the customer stays, goes, or recommends the company to others. A receptionist who fails to answer the phone courteously or promptly may have an adverse affect on a customer's perception of the organization.

In a sales-centric business, everybody needs to have some basic sales training. Everyone should be educated enough to recognize the problems that the company can solve. Then, every employee becomes a conduit for bringing opportunities into the business. A receptionist might meet someone at a party that their company may be able to help. A successful organization will have educated the receptionist to recognize this opportunity. They will also have made the receptionist aware of commissions available for successes initiated by them. While your receptionist may not take the potential customer through the whole sales process, they will be able to take their details and receive their permission to pass them on to an appropriate person within the business.

The point is: the world is too competitive and building pipeline too important to let opportunities go astray. Everybody in your business should be educated to look for these opportunities. As a business owner, if the business is you alone, creating opportunities must be a primary concern. However, if you employ others, it should not be solely down to you. For example, if you employ four other people and each of those four come into contact with 250 others during the course of their everyday lives – at social gatherings, parties, etc. – that brings your company into contact with another 1000 people for no added cost.

UNDERSTANDING YOUR SALES FIGURES

Most business owners would not dream of running a company without having a good understanding of their finances. Without knowing the basics, like their costs and overheads, gross and net profit margins, and cash flow forecasts, it would be extremely difficult to run a business well.

Yet, when it comes to sales, people seem prepared to leave it to chance. Surely, the sales figures are as important as the financial information at your disposal? Without sales, there is no business.

Sales figures must be watched and planned just as people plan their finances. In order to plan sales, you need to understand the life cycle of your business. For example: how many customers do you lose each year and on average, how long do you retain a customer? Once you understand that you are losing 10% of your customers a year and an average customer is retained for three years, you can examine your business cycle and see if there is a way of keeping some of those customers. You can then set a target for retention. For example:

A training company delivers three levels of management training programmes. They tend to deliver one programme, per client, per year. Therefore, after three years they have delivered all of their programmes for a particular client. As they work for many small and medium size organizations, there is not an influx of new people to train at all of their clients. Therefore, about 10% of their customers are lost each year. By being able to explain and understand this figure, the training company may decide to add additional services or new programmes which they feel will be relevant to some of their customers. In this way, they can set a target for selling these new services and retaining a percentage of their client base previously lost.

Examining your existing customer base will also enable you to set targets for up-selling. For example, if 30% of your customers are using your basic service, you may set a target for upgrading 10% of those. Once you have set realistic targets for both retaining and up-selling customers, you will then know how many new customers you will require in order to reach your growth targets.

It is then that you must do your best to understand your sales conversion figures. Every activity undertaken must be measured. This becomes empowering. Once you have a comprehensive understanding of these figures you can really take control of your sales. For example:

You may come to know that 1000 mail shots will convert to 20 responses, 20 responses will convert to four meetings and four meetings will convert to one customer.

Markets fluctuate and evolve and so this is never an exact science. Even when using the same message and channel, you will find that, over time, outcomes will change. However, without even attempting to reach this level of understanding, you will never be in control of your sales process.

IDENTIFYING YOUR PROSPECTS

Once you understand your figures and how many new customers you require, you must decide who to target. This is accomplished by using your Problem Map™. On examining the Problem Map™, you need to ask yourself who is most likely to have the problems that you solve. This should produce some possible targets. You then ask yourself, out of these possible targets, for which audience will solving the problem be most compelling? By answering these questions, you will identify the market places where you should concentrate your efforts.

It is also worth asking yourself a second question: who are the secondary audiences to be affected by these problems? By secondary audiences, we mean people who may not be directly affected by the problems but who will certainly be affected indirectly. For example:

If you sell accounting software, you may decide to target finance directors at companies of a certain size. These will be the people who use the software every day of their lives. However, there will be a secondary audience of people who will not use the accounting software themselves but nevertheless will be affected by it.

Managing directors may not be getting the financial information they require. Similarly, the company's accountant, working with the financial director, might experience the same problem. Therefore, although your primary target might be finance directors, who obviously need information and control over their accounts, also targeting accountants and managing directors may prove fruitful.

Asking yourself which secondary audiences are affected by the problems can open up sales and marketing ideas.

WHAT DO YOUR CUSTOMERS LOOK LIKE?

To ensure that your prospecting is as effective as possible, it is worth trying to profile your customers. Sometimes it will be possible to generalize about certain markets. You may even find, on occasion, that demographic information is available. For example, you may be able to access intelligence that will tell you the average age of a company director is 45. A start up business may have to make certain assumptions regarding their customers, as they will not have sufficient clients to draw any significant conclusions. In this instance, it might be worth undertaking some market research in order to obtain more accurate information.

As a business becomes more established, however, and the customer database grows, one will be able to analyse this in order to learn more about what a typical prospect may look like. This information can be obtained through questionnaires and surveys, registration forms, competitions and just by talking with your customers. Depending on your business, you will have to decide on the information that is worth having. You can then determine the best way of it being acquired. Below are some examples of the type of information that may be relevant.

- What is their sex?
- What is their date of birth?
- Are they married or single?
- What jobs do they do?
- Where do they live?
- What hobbies do they have?
- What holidays do they take?
- What music or sport do they like?
- Do they have a certain political persuasion?
- Which TV channels do they watch?
- Which radio stations do they prefer?
- Do they read certain newspapers or magazines?
- Which websites do they visit?

Clear patterns will not always emerge from this exercise. However, sometimes they will and any commonalities that you find are extremely useful. Remember, selling is about conveying possibility and solving problems and you must be prepared to walk away if you cannot help someone. Therefore, you owe it to yourself to have conversations with the people you are most likely to be able to help, as walking away costs you money.

The more you can target and segment your market place, the more likely it is that you can help the people whom you approach. So if you know that 80% of your customers are golfers, then putting on golf days, advertising in golfing magazines and attending golf clubs, is simple logic.

One must never see a customer one-dimensionally. If they are a business customer, you still need to get to know them on a personal level. Remember, people go to work to fund their personal lives. Similarly, it is important you understand what your consumer clients do for a living. For consumers, work is a place where they may spend the majority of their waking moments; therefore it is a significant factor in their life. Moreover, the dividing line between work and home has been blurred by technology. We can check our e-mails while our children are running around our living room or make a business call with our children in the back of our car.

Over 70% of all UK businesses have no employees and are run solely by the business owner or owners. This blurs the lines still further, as the normal 9–5 workday is no longer relevant to these people. They may take their children to school for 9.00 am and then attend a meeting at 8.00 pm. They may work at home on a Sunday morning and take the children to the park on Sunday afternoon. These small business owners will even make purchases with both their professional and personal lives in mind. For example, they may buy a computer for their home office, which they will use for work, but on which their children will play games. The point is: whether you are in business-to-business or business-to-consumer sales, knowing only a customer's personal

life or professional life is to know only half the person. To really understand your customer, therefore, you need to know both.

PART II: ENGAGING YOUR PROSPECT

- Building pipeline is about creating opportunities in order to get new customers.
- To do this, you have to engage with your prospect.
- To be effective, you must have a compelling story to tell.

In order to sell successfully, you have to be able to tell stories.

When selling intangible services, stories enable you to bring them to life. With intangibles, people need to be able to feel, touch and sense them in a palpable way and stories are a mechanism for making this happen, so giving a vivid account of how you helped another cus-tomer in a similar situation can give a prospect a very real sense of the solution you are suggesting.

On the other hand, when selling tangible items, stories are a way of evoking the intangible aspects of the product. For example, if a cus-tomer is looking at your car, they can already see the quality build and the smart leather interior. However, it will be stories that may help them to picture a wonderful sunny day, cruising through the country with the roof down and the wind in their hair. It may be the intangible solutions the car provides that will be a primary reason for the pur-chase.

There is so much 'noise' out there in the market place. The best way of cutting through that 'noise' is for your story to be compelling. To be compelling, you must be relevant and it is easier to be relevant to a small section of people at any one time. You may have a niche prod-uct or service, or you may have one that appeals to a mass market. By having a clear understanding of the problems that you solve, who you solve them for and what these people look like, you can segment your market into different areas. Targeting your prospects, within the tightest market sectors possible, will give you the best value from the time and money you spend. For example:

An IT company has recognized, because of the experience they have, that they are uniquely placed to solve IT problems for the professional services. However, even though the IT company is now specializing in a particular sector of the market, it will be easier to be relevant and compelling by splitting this sector up still further. Therefore, when engaging with their prospects, they will do better to tell a story and produce literature and other materials specifically for the accountants, architects, solicitors etc., individually rather than trying to address the whole professional services market in one go.

ENGAGING YOUR PROSPECT EMOTIONALLY

Stories, to be engaging, have to touch people on an emotional level. We use our Problem Map™ in order to understand the issues that our potential prospects are likely to have. Concentrating on these issues is the best way of gaining our prospect's attention. However, we must also engage with our prospect on an emotional level. Therefore, it is important to introduce feelings into the messages that we deliver. Whether we are talking with a prospect on the telephone or face to face; via advertising, direct mail or over the Internet, etc., these emotions must be included. So, for example, our first three problems in column one of our Problem Map™ (Table 5.1, page 55) are:

- I am looking for a suitable candidate and cannot find anybody.
- Morale in the office reduces as other staff are overworked.
- I start to lose customers who I let down as we are under resourced.

Inserting emotions into these issues makes them far more powerful.

- **I am struggling** as I am looking for a suitable candidate and cannot find anybody.
- **I am concerned** that morale in the office reduces as other staff are overworked.
- **I am worried** that I am starting to lose customers, who I am letting down as we are under resourced.

Problems often have to be implied, rather than explicitly mentioned. Similarly, feelings may sometimes have to be alluded to; and on other occasions can be spoken about directly. However, without introducing feelings into the messages you communicate with prospects, you are in danger of not fully engaging with them. This is because people often relate more to the emotion a problem causes than to the actual issue itself.

MOVING FROM PROSPECTS TO POTENTIAL CUSTOMERS

A prospect is merely someone you identify as potentially being a user of your product or service. Once these people have been identified, you may try and engage with them. However, they only become a potential customer when they engage with you. They may sign up for an e-mail newsletter on your website or complete a registration requesting further information. They may download a free trial or respond to a free offering you have. Alternatively, they could request a meeting, enter a competition or claim a free gift. Whatever it is, their engagement means some action on their part.

Once an action has been taken by your prospect, they move from being someone with whom you are trying to engage, to someone with whom you have entered a dialogue. This dialogue moves them from prospect to potential customer. It may be that someone becomes a potential customer without ever being identified as a prospect. For example, a word of mouth recommendation may result in a complete stranger requesting a meeting. This meeting will still be due to activity conducted by you; in this case, it may have been giving great customer service. In this scenario, you were not seeking that particular customer; they were looking for you. It is important to note that one may employ prospecting strategies that result in potential customers knocking on your door. These strategies effectively make your business a magnet, attracting new customers, by whatever means, and literally pulling them towards you. For example:

> You may decide to target a specific sector by running a high profile competition with a large prize. This will encourage your potential prospects to engage with you, thus starting a dialogue. Moreover, the word of mouth publicity that your large giveaway encourages makes your business attractive to others who also want to be involved in the excitement. Although by launching the competition and targeting an initial market you made the first move; the giveaway is sufficient and provides enough impetus in creating word of mouth publicity to pull prospects to you rather than you having to hunt them down.

Prospects become potential customers when they participate in the process. Good prospecting is all about encouraging people to participate. Putting a process in place, that encourages participation, is a challenge for the modern day business. For example:

> A potential customer may be encouraged to respond to a mailer by the promise of a free gift. The free gift may stimulate their interest further so they register on your website. Registration may mean they receive an information booklet about their given area of interest and this booklet might promote the idea of them attending a seminar. Their attendance may be the first transaction that takes place as it is a chargeable seminar. Further developments at the seminar then lead your customer to other purchases.

One must not lose sight of the fact that, all the way through any process, we must be conveying possibility, making suggestions as to the problems we can solve and, maybe, even solving some of the smaller problems before a purchase has been made, thereby demonstrating competence.

How many touch points or contacts there should be throughout this process and the time scales in which this process takes place will depend on the product or service you are selling. A software solution costing millions of pounds may involve a process that takes years. On the other hand, an inexpensive and low risk product may involve a process that is almost instant.

Measuring your success, at the varying stages of your process, is vitally important. For instance:

> You may know that from every 200 potential customers who sign up to a newsletter, 20 will attend a seminar. Of those, five will sign up for a further training course; one of whom will become an ongoing customer.

Again, it is about knowing your figures. Once you do, it is more likely you will be able to achieve sales targets. These figures will also be your metric by which you can continually try to refine and improve your process.

Routes to Market

There is an abundance of routes to market and ways to make contact with prospects. Companies often undertake activities which never impact on their bottom line. Before putting resources into anything, asking yourself how it will ultimately help to develop sales makes it less likely that you will waste your time and money. When examining the avenues available, another first important factor to take into consideration is how cost effective a particular route will be for your business. You have to consider what an average order is worth and how much profit it generates. You then start to understand how much you can afford to spend on customer acquisition and the expected return on investment. Of course, if you take into account the lifetime value of a customer, you will always be able to afford to spend more on their acquisition. However, you will also have to watch your cash flow. Even if you will receive a return on investment over a customer's five year lifetime, they are unlikely to pay for five years' service up front.

When choosing your routes to market you must be careful to ensure that they reflect your brand and ESP. For example, if yours is a luxury brand aimed at high net worth individuals, distributing door-to-door flyers, even in the right area, would not be appropriate.

Once you have an understanding of the relevant activities you can afford to undertake, you need to develop an integrated strategy. An integrated strategy means using a variety of complementary routes to market to the same target audience. Relying solely on one route to market will not prove as effective as having an integrated approach. This is because different prospects will respond positively to varying approaches. Therefore, a prospect who never looks at their direct mail may meet you at a networking event. Alternatively, someone who never attends networking events may respond favourably to an advert in their professional journal.

An integrated strategy will also provide for the fact that a prospect will, most likely, need to be exposed to a message many times before they choose to act. So having already seen various adverts in their professional journal, they may respond favourably to your direct mail. Then again, having met you at a networking event, a prospect may decide to take up the offer that you mentioned was featured on your website. For a small business, working within a tight market place can be very effective. Even with limited resources, one can become well known and recognized within a small geographical area or particular market sector.

It is worth noting that using separate routes to market to distinct audiences is not an integrated strategy. Telemarketing to accountants, while sending a direct mail to solicitors and advertising to financial advisors might demonstrate a hive of activity, but it is not integrated and will not be as effective.

This chapter lists a variety of routes to market that, as a business owner, you may find useful:

ADVERTISING

Advertising in the press, in the cinema, on billboards, on the web, over radio or on TV can be a good way of reaching an audience. Mass advertising generally works best for big brands. It can also be an effective mechanism for establishing a new brand, but of course, this will need a lot of resource. For a small business, highly targeted advertising to niche markets is often where this medium works best. To get the most out of a highly targeted advertisement, it is worth asking yourself what you want your prospect to do next. Having a call to action on an advertisement also makes it much easier to track its effectiveness.

ALLIANCES

Who else is targeting the same marketplace as you? For example, if you deliver software for sales departments, you may be able to establish an alliance with a training company who also targets that audience. Maybe you can establish links on each other's websites, organize a joint seminar or share costs on promotional material. You could also share your respective customer databases with each other, immediately creating a wealth of new opportunities. The right alliances can also provide an organization with added credibility in the eyes of their different customers.

COMPETITIONS AND PROMOTIONS

Giving people the opportunity to win something, get money off or receive something extra with a purchase is a good way of encouraging people to participate. One must be careful, however, not to devalue your core offering. For example, for a consultant charging for their time, they may give away a free e-book they have written. This gives potential customers something of value which demonstrates expertise and does not undermine the chargeable service they provide.

DIRECT MAIL

Direct mail is a vehicle with which everyone is familiar. It can work extremely well if you have a brand that the customer base you are mailing will recognize. This will either be because you are a famous brand or, alternatively, it may be a mail sent out to existing customers who will therefore know who you are. If however, there is no brand recognition, direct mail traditionally gives a very low response rate.

In order to make it work, it must be compelling. This is most likely if you use a direct mail piece to target a very specific market. Remember, the idea of a mailer is to start engaging with a prospect, therefore, it will need to contain a call to action. What do you want them to do next and what value will they get doing it?

Depending on the order value of your product, you may consider a high-impact mailer. For example, sending someone a bouquet of flowers, a basket of fruit or a luxury item such as earrings is very likely to get their attention. In most cases, the cost will, of course, be prohibitive, but for high-value sales, it may be worth considering.

DOOR-TO-DOOR LEAFLETING

Door-to-door leafleting is a relatively inexpensive way of targeting a large amount of people in a specific geographical area. Although response rates are traditionally low, it can still produce a return on investment as the outlay is fairly small. This medium is most relevant when you have a product or service with mass-market appeal. You must also make sure you have a brand that is appropriate to be marketed in this way.

E-MAIL MARKETING

Sending e-mails to people from whom you do not have permission is SPAM and is ineffective. However, sending e-mails to existing customers in order to give them ongoing value, keeping your company in their thoughts and on occasion up-selling to them, is worthwhile. Having mechanisms in place to capture e-mail addresses, which you can then use, is a good idea. For example, you may encourage people to log into your website with their e-mail address in order to receive something of value. Alternatively, you may run a competition to win something which people enter via e-mail.

EXHIBITIONS

Exhibitions are normally a costly way of marketing a business. Not only is there the stand itself but also the time spent out of the office and in preparation. One must also ensure that an appropriate amount of time and resources are allocated to following up the enquiries the exhibition generates, otherwise it will all be to no avail. Exhibitions will always generate a degree of wasted enquiries. Many people get caught up in the excitement of the day, expressing interest in products and services. However, when they get back to their office and back to reality, their interest dissipates as fast as it came. Despite all this, targeted exhibitions can put you in front of the right audience and present the opportunity to meet prospects who you would not see any other way. Exhibitions can be fruitful but must be carefully considered.

NETWORKING

Networking is about making connections. You can never know too many people. The more people who are aware of your product or service, the better. By having a large network, you become valuable to others. You will find you will often know a supplier who you can recommend to a client and you will be able to introduce people to one another, within your network, to facilitate business for them. Everyone you help will be grateful and in turn will also help you.

With networking, the more you give to others, the more you will get back. There are many networking groups around, meeting at all times of the day, from breakfast to evening. Many of these general business groups will prove useful and can be found by searching on the web in your area. For example; a very good on-line networking platform, which also has offline meetings, is www.ecademy.com.

If your target market is in a particular sector, one should also network where these individuals go. For example, if you work with financial services companies, attend their seminars, lunches, exhibitions and other gatherings. Joining their relevant associations and attending those meetings may also prove worthwhile.

PODCASTS AND BLOGS

A blog that is content rich should be picked up by search engines and, therefore, will bring you greater presence on the web. If it becomes established, it can also position you as an expert in your field. Similarly producing podcasts can position you as an expert in your field and may be passed on to others.

When using these mediums you must always be thinking about the action you are encouraging recipients to take. You must also ensure you are always delivering value.

PROMOTIONAL ITEMS

Promotional items can be effective at keeping you in the mind of customers and making others aware of your brand. When choosing promotional items it is important to ensure they fit in with your company ethos. Of course, the more value you can provide with any item, the more likely it is that it will be kept and used.

PUBLIC RELATIONS

There are so many TV and radio stations, magazines, newspapers and websites available today. Many of them specialize in particular markets or geographical areas. All of these are searching for good stories and good content. Put yourself in the editor or station controller's shoes. Find out the sort of material they favour. Once you understand this, it will be possible to generate stories of interest. In doing so, you can develop good relationships with these people, which will make it easier to continue getting good PR in the future.

Writing letters to the editor or phoning in to radio programmes can also be a good way of generating publicity.

PUBLIC SPEAKING

There is an array of business groups, associations and organizations that have regular meetings and are looking for speakers. If you can deliver a speech with good content, to a relevant audience, it helps to establish you as an expert in your field and can be an excellent way of generating business. Organizing your own seminars can also be effective. In order to ensure your subject is compelling, it is worth targeting a seminar aimed at a very tight market sector.

REFERRALS

You should be asking your customers, and people with whom you engage, if they know anybody who may be able to use the products or services you provide. This can be formalized by putting in place a referral scheme. This works by encouraging people to make referrals and offering them incentives to do so.

When devising your referral scheme, you must ensure you are delivering value to those people passing you referrals. If you are giving away a gift, what problems does it solve and how does it help the referrer? Making people feel a part of something special can be very effective. For example, once a referral is made, the referrer could automatically become part of a club where they receive free gifts and are invited to exclusive events, thus encouraging further referrals down the line.

TELEMARKETING

Telemarketing can work well as an initial way of engaging a prospect. However, you must ensure your call is highly relevant. It, therefore, works best when applied within very tight markets. You must also plan carefully so you can start delivering value immediately, thereby encouraging participation from the prospect. It is also vital that you have a process in place and you understand what happens after the phone call in order to get maximum benefit from your efforts.

Telemarketing can also be a very cost effective way of keeping in touch and engaging with your existing clients. If undertaken properly, it can be a good way of solidifying relationships and up-selling.

VIRAL MARKETING

The idea behind viral marketing is that you deliver a message that will be forwarded from person to person and, therefore, it almost develops a life of its own. This puts your message in front of people you would otherwise never reach. In order for this to be achieved, the message normally delivers a highly valuable piece of information or needs to be extremely funny. There are numerous examples of e-mails, short films and cartoons that have literally been e-mailed around the world.

WEB MARKETING

More and more people are searching on-line for products or services that they require. Therefore, spending money on the web, whether it is pay-per-click advertising or search engine optimization, etc., can be very cost effective.

Bear in mind that most people looking for something specific already recognize a problem that they have. If you ensure your website directly answers those concerns, it is more likely to keep your prospects' attention. You can only sell one thing at a time; yet so many websites contain a variety of different products and services solving different issues. It may be worthwhile, therefore, having a series of smaller websites than one huge site. Alternatively, you may decide to keep your main company website, but have several micro sites addressing specific issues.

For example: if I am looking for a new TV, your website addressing just this problem may come up high on a search engine. The front page may be '10 things to look for when choosing a new TV'. This page conveys possibilities to customers and arms them with information to solve their problem. By delivering this first, you give a potential customer instant value and therefore start to elicit their trust. The rest of the website can then be dedicated to the TVs you sell. A link from that site may then take a customer to your main site where you not only have TVs, but DVDs, cameras and computers, etc.

However, if they were directed to this site in the first instance it may not have been specific enough to hold their attention. By having a series of micro sites, tackling specific issues, it will be easier to engage with a customer when they initially visit.

WORD OF MOUTH MARKETING

If you deliver a good product or service, provide excellent client support and develop solid relationships with your customers, they will no doubt talk about you positively on occasion. This, over time, is likely to result in new business.

It is possible, however, to run promotions and campaigns that get people talking about your business. For example, you may send something to customers that they are likely to show others or pass on; or you could hold events or pull stunts that are a little unusual or exciting and will encourage others to talk about your business. Your own creativity is the only ceiling on what can be done in this area of marketing.

WRITING ARTICLES

Writing articles for relevant websites, newspapers and magazines can be a good way of getting business and establishing yourself as an expert in your field. There are so many titles and forums in the market place and many of these are looking for good material. You may be a graphic designer with several solicitors as clients. In this scenario you could offer articles to the media aimed at both graphic designers and solicitors, respectively. For instance, for a legal journal, you may write an article on the challenges facing solicitors in today's competitive market and how they can stand out from the crowd.

Whichever routes to market you choose to utilize, you need to engage your customer. Always think in terms of your Problem Map™ and what problems you solve for the potential audience. This will help you communicate in line with your buyer's motivations. To be really effective, the problems will usually need to be implied in the message, rather than explicitly mentioned. Finally, remember that all of these routes to market are used to enable you to start a dialogue with a potential customer. You must, therefore, ensure that they always know what to do next (a call to action) and you must deliver sufficient value that they will want to continue participating in the process that you have begun.

Empowering your Buyer 10

Training courses and materials devoted to selling will often refer to the seller's fear of rejection. That is, the apprehension that comes with the possibility of being told 'no' and how it can affect one's performance.

It is no surprise this happens when using the traditional transactional sales model which makes selling a zero sum game, and all about winning or losing. When using the ideas within Sales Therapy®, this should no longer be of concern. Sales Therapy® is about conveying possibilities and solving problems. Ultimately, it is about helping people. Sometimes, you will be able to help, on other occasions, you may not. Either way, Sales Therapy® recognizes the inherent value for the customer in the sales process, which makes any dialogue worthwhile.

Rather than any fear the seller may have, it is actually the buyer's fears that should be of primary concern; for it is these that can become a real barrier in the sales process. It is a widely held myth that people do not like being sold to, but they like to buy. Therefore, we are told, we should not sell to people; instead we must help them buy. While it is accurate that the emphasis should be on helping people buy, rather than selling; the premise that people 'love to buy', is absolute nonsense.

It is true, that people often have a tremendous feeling of satisfaction after they have made a purchase, assuming that they feel content with the decision they have made. As buyers, we will often be excited to use a product or service that we have just purchased and will gain enjoyment out of something new. Eventually, of course, the novelty dissipates.

Meanwhile, when we first decide to make a purchase, we are often enthused by the array of possibility facing us. So, for example:

> Once we have decided to purchase a new car, we get very excited by the options that we have. Exploring these possibilities and imagining ourselves driving any number of these vehicles can be very enjoyable. However, when it comes to the actual buying and the process of having to make a decision, our mood changes.

We all have fears that make the actual process of buying appear to be daunting. This is especially true when we are purchasing consumer products; where we are investing a lot of our money, like a car; or in business, when we are making decisions that may have far reaching ramifications. It is important to understand that although we may be excited to begin the journey of making a purchase, and we may be pleased when that journey is completed, making a decision is rarely an enjoyable experience. Accepting the widely held generalization that people 'love to buy' misses this point and can prevent us from selling effectively, for it is an assumption that, most of the time, is wrong.

WHAT DO BUYERS FEAR?

As we are all buyers, it should be easy to understand the emotions they have. Overall, buyers have a fear of failure. That is, that any buying decision they make will be unsuccessful. This fear of failure consists of four main concerns:

1   **The fear of paying too much:**
We have all bought something, only to discover that it is available cheaper elsewhere. Although paying more does not necessarily mean we have been ripped off, it nevertheless makes us feel foolish. Moreover, few of us have money to waste and therefore we are concerned not to let this happen.

2   **The fear of being left disappointed:**
We have all been left disappointed by purchases we have made. Either the product or service has not performed in the way we were led to believe, or it has not met our expectations. This can be because we have been misled by a sales person or a company's literature. Sometimes it might be that our own expectations are unreasonable. Having all had experiences where we have felt let down after a purchase, we are wary of allowing the situation to occur again. The bigger the purchase, the greater our concerns normally are.

3   **The fear of being laughed at or criticized:**
Our emotions play a large part in most of the buying decisions that we make. It is because of this that our purchases are a reflection of who we are. The shops we go to, the clothes we wear and the cars we drive all say something about us as individuals. We worry about remarks that colleagues, friends and family may make to us. These people will, therefore, affect our buying decisions. Have you ever picked up an item of clothing in a shop and then placed it back on the peg because, at the back of your mind, you could hear one or two choice remarks that certain friends would make?

In business, these concerns manifest themselves in other ways. Most people go to work to avoid loss and are, therefore, risk averse. They are terrified of making decisions that will be deemed wrong by colleagues or bosses. A bad decision could cost someone a pay rise, promotion or ultimately, their job. The opinion of others is always an important consideration in the work place.

4   **The fear of change:**
Human beings, by their very nature, are conservative creatures. Even the biggest risk takers among us do not find change easy. This is because we are creatures of habit. We have to be. There are

so many thought processes involved in just getting up, having a shower, cleaning our teeth, making breakfast and getting to work that, if we did not undertake these activities habitually, we could not function. The result of this is that we become very comfortable with familiar patterns of behaviour and when these are challenged, we find it very unsettling.

To illustrate this, think about your own home:

> Have you ever considered that regardless of how many seats you have in your living or TV room, you invariably sit in the same chair? In fact, if someone with whom you live sits in your chair, you are likely to ask them to move.
>
> What is more, if a friend comes round and unknowingly sits in your chair, although most of us would be too polite to say anything, you find yourself feeling slightly uncomfortable in a different seat. Is it not rather absurd, that in our own living room, one tiny piece of the planet that is ours, we can feel uncomfortable because we are merely sitting in a different chair? What is more, however comfortable we become in the new seat, as soon as our friend leaves, we will immediately revert back to sitting in our favourite chair once more.

People do not like change and, more often than not, when we are selling, our solution will involve some. Sometimes, people will maintain an undesirable situation rather than go through the pain of change. Only when they perceive this undesirable situation to have become unbearable, do they then embrace new ideas more positively.

Unless we take all these fears that the buyer has into consideration, and do our utmost to alleviate them, we will never be successful at selling. Even when we have the right solution, for the right customer, at the right time, these fears can prevent a purchase being made. Understanding how to allay these fears is key to being able to sell our products or services successfully.

MAKING THE BUYER FEEL COMFORTABLE

In order to facilitate the buying process, you have to establish the right environment. This means creating a situation where the buyer is willing to consider new ideas and discuss options. If your buyer is not relaxed enough to be open minded, then the situation is not conducive to selling.

It is, therefore, vital that you, as the seller, do your best to ensure your buyer feels comfortable. The Sales Therapy® model enables you to do this. We have all been the victim of sales people totally fixated upon the transaction and staring at us with '£' signs in their eyes. We do not feel they have any regard for our interests whatsoever, and this gives us a sense of unease.

The opposite, therefore, is also true. If you do not focus on the transaction, but concentrate only on conveying possibility and solving problems, you will come across as someone who is not motivated by their own self-interests. Moreover, if you adhere steadfastly to the conviction that if you cannot help your potential customer, you will walk away, then you ensure you are 'acting in their interest'.

Just as a customer will have a sense of the self-regarding sales person with '£' signs in their eyes, they will also sense the seller who has integrity and puts their interests first. By concentrating on your customer's interests, and conveying possibilities and solving problems, you are more likely to add value and create an environment where your buyer starts to relax and feel comfortable. The situation then becomes a self fulfilling prophecy. The more relaxed and comfortable your buyer is, the more receptive they are likely to be to your suggestions. What is more, they are likely to open up and contribute to the process in a positive way. The more your buyer does this, the deeper your understanding of their situation will become. This, in turn, will mean your suggestions are likely to be even more relevant and therefore, you will provide increasing value.

UNDERSTANDING RISK

Paying too much for something, being left disappointed, laughed at or criticized and the fear of change are all risks the buyer takes if they choose to make a purchase. It is, therefore, worth evaluating your own product or service against these concerns to see how you can minimize the effects of the risks your buyer faces. The more you can do to alleviate these risks, the less likely it is that they will become a barrier to making the sale. For example:

- Many retailers offer a price match. That is, if you find a product cheaper elsewhere, they will refund the difference. This helps to diminish any price concern the buyer has.
- A money-back guarantee can dispel the fear of being left disappointed, as any purchase that proves unsatisfactory can be returned.
- Testimonials from previous contented customers can start to allay concerns around the thoughts and opinions of friends or colleagues. These testimonials and endorsements demonstrate that the buyer is in good company when making a decision to purchase.
- Free 'time limited' trials of products or services can ease someone into a purchase. The trial gives a buyer the opportunity to use the product or service before making an extensive commitment. As it becomes familiar, the change that will take place by committing to the purchase, long term, seems less daunting.
- Having a get-out clause, so a customer can exit a contract at any time, or guaranteeing a minimum performance level, can also be effective in reducing perceived risk in the customer's eyes.

Of course, there are any number of ways to take perceived risks out of a purchase. What is appropriate for one business will not be relevant for another. Any way you choose to lessen the risk for a customer must be commercially viable for you. Whatever assurances you decide to build into your product or service, do not underestimate the importance of planning this security into your offering.

THE IMPORTANCE OF EMPOWERMENT

> Picture yourself walking into your favourite clothes retailer. An assistant approaches asking; 'Can I help you?' At this point, many of us will automatically raise our hand replying, 'No thanks, I am just looking.'

Why do we do that?

The reason is, we fear that we will lose control of the buying process. This fear is an artificial one. High street retailers are not hard-sell organizations and most do not pay their shop assistants a commission, but a flat hourly rate. What is more, most retailers will allow the return of an item with a valid receipt. However, none of this matters. The thought of being accompanied by a shop assistant who may try and sell us items that we do not want, or who could talk us in to a purchase we later regret, is enough to precipitate the automatic response that we give: 'No thanks, I am just looking.'

A customer who does not feel in control of the situation in which they find themselves will be defensive and apprehensive. They certainly will not be of a mind set conducive to having an open and honest discussion. Unless a customer approaches the seller and asks for their help, they will always perceive that the person selling is in control of the situation. Even when approaching a seller, they may not always feel in control.

When selling, so many people retain this perceived control. They sell **at** their customer, trying to persuade them to buy their product or service. The customer, feeling defensive and uneasy, is unlikely to be receptive to questions or open-minded to any suggestions. In fact any recommendations are likely to result in an array of objections, many of which will be a defence mechanism. The whole process becomes adversarial. This is all wrong.

The reality is:

> **The person selling never has ultimate control because a buyer always has the final say as to whether they want to purchase or not.**

When a sales person does bully someone into making a purchase, it will often result in an item being returned, a cancelled order or a disputed invoice. The seller does not have control. However, any feeling a buyer has that the person selling is in control will prevent an honest discussion taking place because it will produce a defensive reaction within them. Therefore, it is vital that the seller empowers their prospective customer as quickly as possible and throughout the sales process.

The quicker the power that the buyer already has (but does not feel like they have) is given back to them by the seller, the quicker they will start to relax and be willing to have a decent conversation.

As buyers, we do not want to be sold **at**; but sold **with**. In an age where we have more choice, knowledge and control over our lives, compared with previous generations, we do not respond favourably to being assaulted by someone's sales messages.

Conversely, when we participate in the sales process, the decisions we reach are not the seller's decisions but our own. Thus, empowering a buyer begins to negate any requirement for fancy closing techniques. If the seller decides on the appropriate solution, they will have to work extremely hard to convince their prospective customer that it is the right one. However, if the buyer decides the outcome of a discussion for themselves, they will not need convincing that the conclusion arrived at is correct.

GIVING YOUR CUSTOMER CONTROL

Imagine going back to our favourite clothes retailer. This time, you are somewhat taken aback when the shop assistant says the following; 'I wonder if you can help me? I am really sorry to disturb you, but my supervisor is over there and has been berating me all morning. I really don't care whether you buy something or not, but do you mind if I walk around the store with you?'

There is a good chance, on receiving this request, you will agree. This may be because you take pity on the assistant. However, it might also be due to one key phrase the assistant said which was; 'I really don't care whether you buy something or not'. As soon as the sales assistant says this, they transfer any perception of control straight to you. By stating that they do not care whether you make a purchase, the implication is that it is entirely your decision.

Of course, the reality is, it was always your decision. However, as buyers, that is often not the way we feel. By stating this fact so clearly, the control, in this instance, is placed firmly with you, the buyer.

I am not suggesting that you approach every sales meeting by telling your potential customers you do not care whether they buy or not. Neither am I suggesting that every retailer adopts this policy. By definition, if it were to become policy it would not be genuine and, therefore, would become another tired sales trick. The principle, however, is sound.

Let us assume you accepted the assistant's request. You start to relax, as you feel firmly in control of the situation. You strike up a relationship, making small talk as the assistant helps you locate the items for which you are looking. Whilst you are trying on different items of clothing, they make suggestions as to other items on sale that would complement them. Being comfortable and feeling in control, you respond favourably and are willing to explore the assistant's suggestions. In this situation, you may very well end up purchasing many more items than you originally anticipated.

Inadvertently, by empowering us, the assistant created an environment conducive to buying. We felt relaxed and when the assistant conveyed possibilities to us, we were happy to explore their recommendations. These suggestions helped solve the problems of matching items to create outfits, while fulfilling our other requirements of status and aspirations. Many of the risks of purchase were already dissipated as we were aware that the retailer will allow us to return any items with a valid receipt. Therefore, once we had been empowered, an almost perfect environment for buying had been created.

It is vital that you empower your potential customers. If they perceive you have control, they will feel vulnerable. This results in them being apprehensive and defensive. In this state, they will not be open minded and willing to explore different ideas. Once you empower your prospect and give them the sense of being in control, the feeling of vulnerability starts to disappear and they relax. It is much more likely they will then be willing to have an honest discussion.

You empower your customer in two ways:

1   You must ensure your demeanour is not too aggressive or forthright. You can have strong ideas and opinions but they must be projected in a convivial manner. You can say all the right things, but if your body language and mannerisms are overpowering, your customer will still feel vulnerable.

2   When introducing ideas and solutions to your customer, you can
     begin by giving them control of the situation first. Little phrases
     such as:
     - 'I'm not sure if this is relevant, but …'
     - 'I don't know, tell me what you think of this …' and
     - 'This is only a suggestion, but what do you think of …'
     immediately puts your customer in a position of strength.

The implication of these statements is that you are asking their opinion, as you are not entirely sure of the most appropriate solution for
them. By asking for your customers' views, rather than simply stating
your own opinions, you achieve two things:

1   You allow your customer to have control, as by asking their opin-
     ion and questioning the relevance of your particular idea you
     imply that the decision is up to them. Of course, the decision is
     always up to them.
2   By asking, rather than telling, your customer about a solution, you
     encourage them to participate in finding the answers.

On many occasions, your customer will, in fact, make suggestions or
have ideas that you may never have introduced into the conversation
but, nevertheless, you can accommodate. In this way, you are facilitating a buying process, rather than selling. The customer will often sell
the solution to themselves. Moreover, as it is the customer's solution,
it is much more likely to be the most suitable for them. It will not be
necessary to convince and persuade your customer it is the right solution, for they may never have bought your solution, but they will buy
their own.

As the seller, you may have the expertise and the knowledge of a market
place and what is possible. You may steer your customer in the right
direction and guide the conversation. However, comments such as:

- 'I'm not sure if this is right for you, but …'
- 'Tell me, do you think this may be suitable …'

empower your customer and encourage their participation. In this way, you become partners trying to explore ideas and solve a problem together, rather than combatants on opposite sides of the fence, which so often happens in the traditional sales model.

Remember, ultimately the customer is always in control. All you are doing is allowing them to recognize this. In other words, their situation does not change, only their awareness of it does. If they are not conscious of the control they have, it will be very difficult to have a good conversation with them. Then, by asking rather than telling your customer, you encourage their participation. This approach is not only more effective, but makes it more likely the solution will be right for them. Ultimately, you must remember that if you cannot help, you will walk away. By keeping this in mind, you will be able to have good conversations with customers, make sales and always keep your integrity intact.

Understanding your Purchasers

11

Regardless of whether you are selling to consumers or businesses, there will always be a buying process.

In order to be successful, this must be understood. For example:

> In a consumer environment a family may have their own system for reaching decisions. Firstly, a wife may conduct some initial research and identify two or three possible suppliers. It may be that her husband then investigates those suppliers further and they finally make the buying decision together.

To understand the buying process, one has to recognize who is involved and the extent of that involvement. For example, in a family, it may be a child who precipitates a purchase for their birthday. However, it will be their parents who then source the supplier and make the purchase.

The purchasers' attitude to risk will also affect their buying process. They may be very meticulous and ensure they have checked all the finer details. Alternatively, they may be prepared to take more of a gamble. The attitude the purchasers have to risk will change depending on the purchase. Most people, when buying a house, will want to be thorough. This may also be required by a bank, who may be lending them the money. On the other hand, when downloading a new album from the Internet, for little cost, a purchaser may be very willing to buy without listening first, therefore, exposing themselves to a risk, albeit, on a relatively minor item.

A buying process can comprise one person on their own, or involve many different people. Consumer purchases will often have very few people involved. For example, the person who goes to the supermarket to undertake the food shopping, for the family, may be the sole decision maker and in the majority of cases will decide on a purchase then and there. In a small business, employing only a few people, it may be the business owner who, single handedly, makes most purchasing decisions. When selling to larger businesses, you may find that buying decisions are made by a number of different people and the process becomes a lot more complicated.

Regardless of the number of people involved in the buying process, whether it is one or one hundred, you must remember that every single person will have their own concerns based on one or more of the following:

- Their personal agenda: their own concerns relating to their private life.
- Their professional agenda: their concerns relating to their career.
- Their practical agenda: the tangible characteristics the product or service must have.
- Their emotional agenda: their opinions and thoughts based on their feelings.

These different areas of concern can present themselves in a variety of ways. Let us take, for example, a small business owner buying a laptop:

- Their personal agenda is that they want a laptop that the children can also use when required.

- Their professional agenda is that the laptop is capable of running programmes compatible with a major supplier.
- Their practical agenda is that it is of sufficient screen size and keyboard size that they are comfortable using and carrying the machine.
- Their emotional agenda is about looks and style. They want a laptop that they will be happy using in front of colleagues.

This scenario is just as relevant in large businesses. For example, a sales representative choosing a new company car:

- Their personal agenda will be that their husband likes the car and there will also be sufficient room for their two children.
- Their practical agenda will be that it is an automatic as they do a lot of driving in heavy traffic.
- Their professional and emotional agenda will be a compromise of driving a car that fulfils their requirements of status and aspirations, while, at the same time, not being too ostentatious, as this might have an adverse affect on the customers they visit.

Potentially, if there are 20 people involved in a decision, there can be 20 different personal, professional, practical and emotional considerations.

Understanding the different concerns of your potential customers is vitally important and can sometimes defy your own assumptions. You must not take anything for granted or at face value. Instead, you need to investigate the different criteria those involved in the buying process have. The example below, of a procurement department in a large PLC appears simplistic; it is, nevertheless, the type of mistake that regularly occurs when selling.

You may assume a procurement department will be aiming to obtain the lowest price possible for a particular item. However, this procurement department is targeted on savings rather than price. In other words, if the retail price is £100 and the department negotiates to buy it for £50, it has made a £50 saving. In this scenario, the head of procurement may be more inclined to purchase the item for £50 than a similar item priced at £40 by a competitor. Although the second item is £10 cheaper, its initial cost was only £80, thus, if the procurement department obtains the second item, they have only made a saving of £40 rather than £50 and will achieve less commission. Had the second company understood this, they may well also have priced their item at £100 at the beginning of the negotiations. If they had, thereby realizing a saving of £60, the head of procurement may well have chosen them to be their supplier.

Because the different people involved in a buying decision will have various agendas, you may have to draw up a Problem Map™ for every position. For example:

The CEO's agenda may be different from their senior management. The CEO's primary concern may be to keep the senior management team content; meanwhile, some members of the senior management team may be looking to make their mark within the organization. The users of the software may also have a say in the decision. Their focus may be on the immediate problems the software is being purchased to solve.

A Problem Map™ for each person or department, within the company, will help clarify the issues and, therefore, messages that are relevant.

You will also have to analyse the risk, of a purchase, for every position or department within the company. For example, people do not like change, so you will need to consider the ramifications of a purchase, in terms of change.

- For a CEO, there may be no personal change. They are not going to be using the product and it is not going to have any bearing on them.
- For the product's users, it might mean a dramatic change, thereby potentially creating a certain amount of resistance at that level.

All the risks need to be analysed. For example, buyers are scared of being derided or laughed at by colleagues. So, if someone in middle management is tasked with making the decision, there may be certain risks that need considering.

- Are they going to be anxious about what the CEO or another director is going to say?
- Are they going to be worried that they will be ridiculed by the people they are managing?
- Who could potentially be disappointed by the purchase if it doesn't work out?
- Who is afraid of looking stupid if the company pays too much for it?

When selling to a very small business or a consumer, it is unlikely that many people will be involved. If you are selling to a large organization, there can be a variety of people involved and the sale can be extremely complex. Drawing up a separate Problem Map™ in order to help understand the emotional, practical, professional and personal agenda for the people involved can be extremely time consuming. If the order value, however, is large enough, it will be worthwhile undertaking this activity.

THE DMU (DECISION MAKING UNIT)

Before one can take into account the considerations of any people involved in a purchase, we have to understand who those purchasers are. When selling to consumers this can be a single individual, two partners, friends or an entire family. For example:

> Take a family moving house. It may be that the head of the household takes it upon themselves to make a purchasing decision on their own. Alternatively, a husband and wife may take the decision together but feel it unnecessary to involve their adolescent children. A different family, however, may feel unable to make a purchasing decision without a husband, wife and children all agreeing together.

The same is true in companies. In a small business, the business owner may make a decision alone or ask trusted colleagues, friends or family for help. As businesses get bigger, there are likely to be other directors, management and users involved. Whatever the combination, decisions will be made by a DMU (Decision Making Unit). A DMU can comprise of a single individual making a decision alone, or a large number of people who will make a decision together.

Thinking in terms of a DMU is a useful mechanism. However, you must not lose sight of the fact that although the DMU is a useful tool, people making decisions may not regard themselves as part of any decision making unit. Decisions will often be influenced by a disparate group of people who, knowingly or unknowingly, will have an effect on any outcome. For example:

Within a company, it may be two directors who make a decision on a purchase, although several other people are involved in influencing their thoughts. If you were to ask the people within the company who makes the decision, they would point at the two directors. However, as the seller, it will be important to recognize the other people who have influence on any deal.

A husband and wife are unlikely to regard themselves as a decision making unit, even though, when making certain purchasing decisions, they could well be. If you were to call a business and ask to speak to the head of the DMU, you are likely to get nowhere. It is therefore a mechanism for us to use internally, rather than something that should ever be mentioned to a potential customer.

THE COMPOSITION OF A DMU

A Decision Making Unit will normally include up to five different types of people. How many there are will depend on whether you are selling to consumers, small or large businesses and the processes they have.

1   The traditional decision maker:
This is the person who has control over the final decision. It will be them who signs off the order, authorizes the purchase, signs the cheque or hands over their credit card. They may be very involved in the purchasing decision, attending any relevant meetings and reading proposals, etc. Alternatively, they may leave it to others to attend meetings and undertake research. They may then ask those that they have delegated a lot of questions before deciding on the purchase.

Sometimes, the person who signs the cheque may not actually be involved in the decision at all. They may be happy to rubber stamp someone else's decision. You must be careful, therefore, and not assume that the person who signs the cheque will make the decision. This may often be correct, but is not necessarily the case.

2   The influencers:

Influencers may not have the authority to sign off, or write a cheque, but their opinion may carry a lot of weight. This is normally because of their expertise or experience in a given area or alternatively because of their position within a company.

A child may bow to a parent because of their experience and, therefore, may be interested in hearing their parent's advice. In business, the HR department may be installing a new software system that will not affect anyone else. Even so, the HR director may seek the IT director's advice due to the expertise they have. Sometimes a person may be drafted in to the decision making process due to their position. So a middle manager may be charged with making a decision. However, they may decide to involve their director for no other reason than the authority they have.

3   Procurement:

Some large companies have procurement departments comprising people who are professional buyers. They may be involved in all company purchases or only purchases over a certain spend. Procurement will often work with other departments, within the company, to reach decisions. They may or they may not have the final decision but will often be involved in negotiations.

4   Gatekeepers:

A gatekeeper is normally thought of as a receptionist, secretary or PA. In reality, anyone you have to go through in order to reach the right people is a gatekeeper. A gatekeeper can have a lot of influence or none at all. Even without any executive powers, a gatekeeper can fail to pass on messages or provide information that can have a great bearing on a decision. A gatekeeper mentioning that they find a particular supplier rude can put a boss or a colleague off a company. Some CEOs are very close to their PAs and will, quite naturally, ask for their opinion of someone they meet. One must be aware of a gatekeeper's influence in a sales process. They may not be deal makers, but they can certainly be deal breakers.

5   The users:
Take a company about to make a large investment in new software for the human resources department. It may be the HR director who has the final say. However, they may bring in the IT director, because of their experience and the CEO because of their authority, into the decision making team. Meanwhile, the HR director's PA, who answers the phone, timetables the meetings and fields the proposals that are presented, will have an influence on events.

There are also the actual users of the product. These are the three people within the HR department who will use the software day to day. The HR director will also be asking for their opinion.

WORKING WITH THE DMU

For a consumer, the buying decision in a supermarket can take moments. At a corporate level, if it is a large investment, with far reaching effects across the whole organization, the process can take years. In a purchase where there are a variety of decision makers, it is unlikely you will be able to spend an equal amount of time with them all. You will, therefore, have to prioritize.

You will have to decide which people have the most influence. For example, amongst the users, there may be those who have been in the department longer and whose opinion is particularly respected. In order to concentrate your efforts most effectively, you need to try to understand how the people involved in the DMU relate to each other. The politics between the different departments and personalities within a company can be vital to the final outcome. You must be aware of this and try and learn as much as you can during visits and communication via e-mail and telephone. Ultimately, it is not something that you will know and, therefore, you will have to ask as many questions as you can.

- How are decisions made?
- Who is involved?
- Who are the main players within the organization and within each department?
- Who would be involved in giving the go ahead?
- What are the buying criteria?
- How will they know when they have made the right choice?

Only by continually asking questions can you begin to understand who a buying decision will affect and who is going to be involved.

If you are selling to a DMU comprising only two people and you are sitting in front of them, it may only take a few questions to ascertain what you need to know. If, however, you are dealing with many people in a large organization, it will take numerous questions and a period of time before you can understand the organization's buying process. You must listen carefully. What is not said can be as important as what is said.

Note who is copied in on e-mails and who is not. Which people are party to what meetings? Sometimes it could be a major influencer or decision maker who does not attend meetings. It may be that you need to try and get them involved in some way, because without them present, it may be harder to get the deal, for, if they are not there, you are relying on their colleagues to sell your solution on your behalf. As they are unlikely to be as effective as you, this scenario is far from ideal.

There are so many different factors to take into consideration when dealing with DMUs. A lot will depend on the company and the type of product or service you are selling. When you do have an understanding of the most important players within a buying process, it is worth looking for an advocate among them, that is, someone who is enthusiastic about your solution and who will be positive in your absence. You will not be present at every meeting and every conversation that takes place. Having an advocate means that someone is putting across your point of view, even when you are not present. In longer sales cycles, it can be quite difficult to keep the momentum going. Having one or two advocates, within an organization, will help to keep your solution on the agenda. Advocates may be willing to also give you critical information as circumstances change or opportunities arise. In complex sales, with many personalities involved, having an advocate within an organization can make all the difference to your chances of success.

THE SALES ORGANIZATION

To be successful, organizations must be customer centric; that is, fully focused on putting the customer first. Selling is about conveying possibility and solving problems. Ultimately, it is about helping people. Therefore, a customer centric organization is also a sales centric organization. In a sales centric organization, everybody has to be involved in selling. You may have a sales person or team dedicated to this part of the business. However, to dismiss selling as an activity that is the sole responsibility of a person or department is imprudent. In a sales centric organization, everyone must accept that they may be called upon to speak to their counterparts in prospective customers' companies in order to facilitate business taking place.

It may be that, as a business owner, you will need to speak to your counterpart at a prospective customer's organization. Whether it be IT director to IT director; or operations director to operations director; a promise will often come across with more authority and sincerity when it comes from the mouth of one's counterpart. This is especially true when dealing with a large contract or purchase where the perceived risk is relatively high. However far the sales team or person take the negotiations, it may need the involvement of others within the organization to secure the business. Perceived risk can dissipate quicker when a business owner of a company shakes another business owner's hand. A sales person's word does not always bring with it the same reassurance or authority as one's counterpart in an organization.

This can permeate throughout a company. Your PA may need to relate to the PAs in your customers' businesses. Understand that selling and customer service go hand in hand and these activities are undertaken on multiple levels.

Selling today is complex and is not necessarily the solitary activity of one department. Sometimes a purchase will involve only a buyer and a seller. Sometimes there will be many people involved. Whatever the size of the DMU, remember that every single person involved in a purchase will have their own professional, personal, emotional and practical agenda.

When the DMU comprises a variety of people, it is essential you ascertain everyone involved. Missing out on the one person who is fundamental to the final decision could cost you the deal. Even though you could help solve their problem, you will not be given the opportunity to demonstrate this. Securing a big ticket sale might not just be down to one person. Be prepared to involve other people in your organization. Transparency is vital. You may need to let counterparts meet. This will provide reassurance to the purchaser and will mean they are more likely to buy. Ultimately, in order for this to happen, everyone within your organization must be competent in selling.

Asking Questions – the Diagnosis

12

PART I: THE DOCTOR/PATIENT RELATIONSHIP

- Every purchase solves a problem.
- The problem belongs to your customer.
- Ultimately it is up to them to solve it.
- All you can do is assist.

> Your doctor prescribes a course of tablets, but whether you take them and complete the course, is up to you. It is outside of your doctor's control. If you are ill, you will go to your doctor who may provide a solution to remedy the problem. It may then require you to go to a pharmacy, pay for a prescription and follow the instructions. You may have had help, but ultimately, it is you who must take action to solve the problem.

It is exactly the same in selling. The seller may make recommendations and give advice, but it is up to the customer to take action to solve the problem.

A sales person asking questions is no different from a doctor making a diagnosis. You must learn from your customer because if you do not understand their reality in its entirety, you cannot make any recommendations that are appropriate or worthwhile.

During your sales diagnosis, your customer will gain an understanding and awareness of their situation, which perhaps they did not have prior to your meeting. You may then provide them with some recommendations and options, after which it is up to them.

Asking questions, therefore, is a fundamental part of the sales process. It allows you to gain an understanding of your customer's reality, while ensuring that they participate in the process, rather than you doing all the talking.

This process is about them; not you:

- People will forget what you say; they are more likely to recollect what they say.
- People will not necessarily believe what you say; they will normally believe what they say.

In the traditional sales model, so much of the sale has been built around the sales person who talks about and presents their product or service, while the client listens. Presenting is ineffective, because it forces you to assume too much about your client's situation. Therefore, inadvertently, the emphasis is on you, not your client. The only way to undertake a presentation that might be effective is to engage with your client and do a diagnosis first. However, a thorough diagnosis negates the requirement for a presentation, rendering the whole exercise futile.

When selling, your role is not to present, but to facilitate a process to give your customer a new awareness of their situation. It is your customer who has the problem and it is, therefore, they who must find the solution. This can only be achieved through an interactive process. You need to ask the right questions to enable you and your customer to learn what is appropriate for them, given their circumstances.

Only by exploring your customer's situation thoroughly will you be able to ascertain whether you can or cannot help them. Selling, by definition therefore, is necessarily reactive. Your customer must talk first in order to explain their position. Only then can you respond. You are no different from a doctor undertaking a diagnosis. Before you can express any opinion, you need to understand the issues, the problems and their ramifications. If you like, you need to know: the origins of the pain, where it hurts, when it hurts, how often it hurts, the issues it is causing, who and what else it is affecting, and what they hope a solution might achieve. Only then will you be able to make some considered recommendations.

If you have been seeing the same doctor for several years, and have been happy with their advice, you are likely to open up and answer questions when asked. However, if it is your first appointment, you are naturally going to be a little wary. This is no different from a customer meeting you for the first time. It will be easier to get a customer to open up and talk if you already enjoy an existing and ongoing relationship.

This is why sales leads that come by referral are easier to handle. There is already a small amount of trust, instilled in the relationship by the person who has made the referral, whereas a completely cold lead will require more care as the relationship has to be developed from scratch.

DEVELOPING RELATIONSHIPS

Business is driven by relationships. The extent to which a relationship must be developed will depend on the product or service you are selling. An inexpensive purchase may only allow for a one-off meeting. You cannot expect to build a solid relationship in one meeting. However, because the risks of an inexpensive purchase may be small, the relationship may not have to be significantly developed in order for a customer to feel comfortable enough to buy.

On the other hand, if you are selling a big ticket item, there is likely to be more risk associated with the purchase. In this scenario, a relationship may have to be cultivated before an acquisition takes place, but because of the size of the order value, there will probably be more time and money for this to happen.

In order to develop lasting relationships, you need to make friends with your customers. The best way to do this is to find things in common. Do you both have children? Did you grow up in a similar part of the world or in similar circumstances? Do you share the same interests or hobbies? It is not difficult to find something in common with someone, and be able to establish some sort of rapport and relationship with them, over a little bit of small talk. Therefore, asking questions at the beginning of the meeting, by way of small talk, can be invaluable. For example:

- Isn't the weather horrible at the moment?
- Did you see the football yesterday?
- How was your journey?

Any of these types of questions will kick-start a conversation as you settle down and get ready for a meeting. Whether you refer to a news item or anything else of interest, if you have confidence and a friendly demeanour, most people will be willing to engage in a little small talk.

Only talk about things in which you are genuinely interested and about which you have some knowledge. Do not pretend to be someone that you are not. You must be genuine at all times with your customers. Be interested in people. People will perceive when you are genuinely interested in them; the same way as people sense when you are being shallow.

Ultimately, we do business with people we like. If we have a friend who supplies a particular product or service that we require, and they can help us, we will probably look no further. Becoming friends with your customers makes your job more enjoyable and helps to lock out the competition. If someone likes you, they will be predisposed to wanting to use you, if they can. Spending a few moments on a little small talk is a gentle way to start a meeting and also an excellent way to finish one. So, at the end of a meeting, as you collect your items together, you can ask:

- What are you doing over the weekend/summer holidays/Christmas, etc?
- Have you got a busy day ahead?
- Are you doing anything interesting this evening?

Whatever it is, ending a meeting with a little bit of small talk is an amiable way to conclude. It allows you to finish on a personal note and get to know one another a little better, thereby developing a relationship on a deeper level than purely business. Remember, people do not just have professional and practical agendas, but emotional and personal ones as well. Ultimately, people buy from people.

In order to facilitate this, you must ensure you are a genuinely interesting person to know. You will find people will then want to know you, talk to you and enjoy being with you. Watch the news and understand what is going on, read up on related topics. Ensure you have subjects about which you can talk. If you enjoy sports, take an interest and acquire some knowledge. As a business owner, managing staff, suppliers and relationships with customers, you are in the people business. So it is really important to master being a people person.

THE DOCTOR/PATIENT RELATIONSHIP

We open up to a doctor for two main reasons, aside from the possibility of already having on ongoing relationship with them.

1   We believe they are an expert in their field. By virtue of being a qualified doctor, practising out of a reputable surgery, we believe

they know what they are talking about. As long as they reinforce this expectation during our time with them, we are normally happy to take their advice.

Similarly, when selling, we must demonstrate our expertise. This can be alluded to, by ensuring any relevant qualifications are on our business card. They will be noticed by our customer. We should also, at applicable moments during the meeting, refer to articles we have written, speeches given, white papers produced, relevant association memberships, or anything that may position us as an authority on our subject. However, the best way of establishing our expertise is by asking good and pertinent questions that make our customers think about their situation. Not only will we give them confidence that we know our subject, but they will also gain value from the meeting. The more useful our customers find the time they spend with us, the more likely it is that they will consider us an expert.

2 We trust our doctor because we believe they are acting in our interest. That is, they have no particular agenda and are simply there to help.

In the same way, a customer must believe that we are acting in their interests. We instinctively feel uncomfortable when someone is trying to sell to us and we do not feel this is the case. If you genuinely act in your customer's interests, this will normally come across and people will respond positively. They are then more likely to feel comfortable and, therefore, answer questions, so you can have a meaningful discussion.

A doctor will not be able to diagnose a patient if the patient refuses to explain the problem and refuses to describe the symptoms or talk about their lifestyle, even when it is a little bit embarrassing. Similarly, if a potential customer holds back and does not tell you things you really need to know, it is going to be very difficult to find an appropriate solution for them. By demonstrating your expertise and genuinely acting in their interests, you will start to make a potential customer feel comfortable and, therefore, be more likely to open up; in exactly the same way as in the doctor/patient relationship.

PART II: THE FALLACY OF OPEN AND CLOSED QUESTIONS

A fallacy exists around the idea of open and closed questions. It is that by using open questions, as opposed to closed questions, you will get your customer to open up, so you can uncover the information you require. Closed questions are those that only need to be answered with a 'yes' or 'no'. For example:

- 'Are you happy with your current supplier?'
- 'Do you review your contracts regularly?'

The perceived wisdom is that because these questions only necessitate a 'yes' or 'no', they are ineffective at generating further discussion, whilst asking open questions – starting with how, which, where, when, who, what and why – will mean you get more thorough answers to your questions.

While open questions are often better questions to ask, it is simply not true to suggest that open questions open people up and closed questions do not. At the very least, this is a gross over-simplification.

In the first instance, open questions do not necessarily open someone up:

Q: *'How do you sort your suppliers?'*
A: *'On cost.'*

Q: *'Who is responsible for your operation?'*
A: *'Jim.'*

Q: *'What do you normally look for when you source a supplier?'*
A: *'Locality.'*

None of these answers are particularly open, although they are all in response to open questions. Similarly one could ask, 'Do you have good relationships with your current suppliers?' Although this is a closed question, and in theory only needs a yes or no, a customer could choose to respond in a very open and thorough way with something like, 'Well I don't actually and the reason is …' They could then list a plethora of reasons why they are not happy with their current supplier.

The point is this: when you listen to politicians being interviewed, they are often asked closed questions. Interviewers like asking politicians closed questions, for example, 'Isn't it true that crime figures went up last year?' The interviewer clearly knows their facts and really wants the politician to say 'yes' in which case they have them on the ropes. 'Ah! So you agree the crime figures are up!' But of course a politician never answers a closed question with a closed answer, so the reply will often be something like; 'Well actually, I think the real indicator here is this …' and off they go, on a tangent, with a seemingly open answer in response to what was intended to be a very closed question.

Similarly, celebrities being interviewed, on TV or radio programmes, will give an open answer even when the interviewer has asked a closed question. So when the interviewer asks; 'Did you enjoy recording the new album?' A singer will not choose to simply answer 'yes' or 'no', but prefer to respond with a fuller answer, relating well rehearsed anecdotes about the recording sessions.

Q: Why do people like politicians and celebrities, answer closed questions with open answers?

A: **Because it is in their interest** to respond with an open answer, even when they are asked a closed question.

A celebrity is on a TV or radio show to sell their new film, their latest book or their next album and it is in their interest to come across as a personality. They want to make the audience laugh with absorbing stories and to come across as likeable. Therefore, they are not going to give closed answers because it is not in their interest to do so.

In the same way, a politician does not want to give a closed answer. They are there to justify their policies and to prove that they are doing a good job in government, or that they could be doing a better job and should be in government. Therefore, they want to use the airtime in order to put their case across. They are not going to give closed answers because it is not in their interest to do so.

It is exactly the same when we are talking to potential customers. If a customer believes it is in their interest to answer, they will be happy to give an open answer and not offer a closed answer, even to a closed question. If they are not the talkative type and give a limited answer, you can ask a supplementary question. For example:

> Q: *'What are your criteria for sourcing suppliers?'*
> A: *'Cost and location.'*
> Q: *'Can you explain that a little more?'*

If they believe it is in their interest to answer the question, they will answer it as fluently as they possibly can.

On the other hand, it does not matter how many open questions you ask, if someone does not feel it is in their interest to answer the question, you are likely to get closed and evasive answers. Asking open questions may help a conversation flow a little more smoothly, but it is not the panacea to effective questioning when selling. Ultimately, your customer will only give thorough answers to your questions if they perceive **it is in their interest** to do so.

GETTING YOUR QUESTIONS ANSWERED

People will be prepared to answer your questions thoroughly if they perceive it is in their interests to do so. Sometimes, this can be achieved by setting an agenda that demonstrates to your customer that this is the case.

When we visit a doctor, we know that the doctor cannot help us unless we tell them what is wrong. So, when the doctor asks us to describe the problem, we give them a reasonable account; for without this, we understand they will not be able to help.

We can set a similar agenda, as in our doctor analogy, when in a selling situation. This can be achieved by prefacing an initial question in a number of ways:

- 'I don't know if I can help, but perhaps I can ask a couple of questions and we can take it from there?'
- 'In order to see if I can help, can I ask …?'
- 'I don't know if I can help, so can I ask …?'

By starting our questioning with these types of statements, we demonstrate that it is to our customer's advantage to answer them, for the only purpose of the questions is to see if we can help them. Moreover, as it is perfectly logical that we won't be able to help without understanding their situation, you will find that by setting this tone, customers are generally receptive.

However, it is not enough to set the right agenda. People will only want to respond openly to questions which they perceive as interesting or useful for them. Beware, therefore, of starting your questioning with mundane questions that have little relevance for your customer. For example:

> Q: 'How many people do you employ, John?'
> A: '26'

John already knew this and it is not exciting for him. It does not present a new awareness nor is it something that keeps John awake at night. It is just a number.

> Q: 'How long have you been running the company John?'
> A: 'Five years'

Similarly, this is another pedestrian question. It is boring for John, and is of very little significance to the issues that he currently faces. If these are things you need to know, they are questions you can ask much later down the line, when you have already engaged with your customer and the relationship is starting to develop.

You must start by asking questions that are of interest to your customer and which they feel are worth answering. These questions will be related to their areas of concern. They will be the issues about which they are often thinking, and the matters that keep them awake at night. These questions are more likely to help you to help them, by bringing out the pertinent issues and the problems that you may be able to solve.

QUESTIONING WITH PROBLEM MAPS™

A doctor's medical training provides them with the ammunition to ask pertinent questions. If you visit their surgery with a throat problem, they will ask medical questions around issues they know they need to understand. After asking about the immediate symptoms, they might ask a wider set of questions in order to appreciate the full context of the problem. These questions may be regarding lifestyle. So, they may cover areas such as: smoking, exercise, diet, work and whether you are under a lot of stress, etc. It is only after understanding all of these issues that a doctor may start to suggest some solutions.

Just as the doctor has medical knowledge; our Problem Map™ is our knowledge. The Problem Map™ indicates the buyer's motivations and the issues they are likely to be facing. It gives us an understanding of the problems these issues may cause and where we can help and add value. It is the Problem Map™, therefore, that will give us the direction for our questions. By initially concentrating on questions that relate to our Problem Map™ we ensure we ask pertinent questions, rather than ones that are mundane. Using our Problem Map™ as a guide also guarantees we start our dialogue based around problems, rather than solutions.

If we start with solutions straight away:

- We do not know if they are appropriate, and they may well not be.
- Even if they are appropriate, we still have no credibility.

If you visit your doctor and you have no sooner sat down, when, without a thorough diagnosis, you are prescribed to take certain tablets three times a day, even if the tablets are right, we would not have any trust in that doctor. The same applies to sales people with their customers. You have to start talking about their immediate issues; then you can develop those issues, gain a real understanding of their concerns and only then, start to make recommendations.

- You cannot begin a journey at the destination.
- You always need to start at the beginning.
- In selling; this means commencing with problems.

Our Problem Map™ is a guide to the issues a customer may be experiencing. We will not necessarily know which of the issues, if any, are pertinent. We, therefore, should always start our questioning with soft questions, based around the four Headline Problems on the Problem Map™. If our customer then indicates these are indeed issues for them, we can use our Problem Map™ as the basis for delving further.

If we take a look at our Problem Map™ (Table 5.1, page 55) for our imaginary company, Fictional Recruitment, we can start to understand how we achieve clarity in our questioning. So, if we were visiting a potential customer, our first soft question might be:

'How do you recruit staff at the moment?'

Their answer to this may be:

'We handle the process ourselves, internally.'

- Headline problem 1 is 'I am looking for a suitable candidate and I cannot find anybody.'
- Headline problem 2 is 'I am too busy to undertake the whole recruitment process.'
- Headline problem 4 is 'I need someone now and can't wait to undertake the process.'

As all three of these problems relates to time pressure in some way, once we find out the process is conducted internally, our next question might be:

'How long does the process normally take?'

Any answer that alludes to any of the three headline problems that we have then allows us to delve deeper. So for example, our customer may answer:

'The process tends to take a long time, because we are so busy with other things.'

Knowing the resulting problems we have in our Problem Map™ under headline problems 1 and 2, we may then respond by asking how this affects their business.

So, once we start talking about the length of time it takes to recruit, and how busy they are, we may introduce themes based around morale in the office, their customer delivery, and work/life balance; all of which are areas that our Problem Map™ indicates may be affected. If your sole focus is conveying possibility and solving problems, a conversation will often naturally develop as your customer starts to feel comfortable and opens up. This will only happen if you genuinely put the interests of your customer at the heart of what you do.

Of course, the answer to our first soft question, 'How do you recruit staff at the moment?' may have been:

> 'We have three suppliers we currently use.'

This being the case, Fictional Recruitment would then focus their mind on our alternative Problem Map™ (Table 5.2, page 57) which address the issues a company may experience if they have an existing supplier. It is impossible to be prepared for every situation. There will be times when you will simply not be able to help. However, if you have created all the relevant Problem Maps™ for the scenarios pertinent to your business, you will find that you are thoroughly prepared for most occurrences. The experiences you have with customers will feed back into the Problem Maps™, which you must regularly review, therefore ensuring they remain relevant.

EMPATHY AND EMPOWERMENT

It is important to appreciate that you will be touching on issues and areas that may be particularly sensitive to a customer. This will sometimes mean that you need to introduce issues delicately. For example, asking directly, 'Do you find you are letting customers down?' is not particularly diplomatic and, therefore, is a question that may put a customer on the defensive. This may mean the answer is brief and evasive.

It is important, therefore, to empathize with a customer as much as possible. The easiest way of doing this is to demonstrate your understanding of their situation, by referring to other clients who have experienced similar problems. So rather than ask them head on about letting their customers down, you may introduce this idea in a different way:

> *'We have often found that some of our other clients have had difficulties recruiting and have then inadvertently let customers down. They haven't meant this to happen, but they have been understaffed. I don't know if this is relevant, but have you ever experienced this type of situation?'*

Using other customers as an example, to introduce the issue, is less threatening – partly because it is less direct. This approach allows you a degree of empathy with your customer as you are talking about a previous situation you have seen. Finally, by alluding to the fact that other people also experience this problem, you make it less embarrassing, personal and sensitive, thereby making it much easier for your customer to talk on this subject.

When introducing sensitive issues into a discussion, it is possible for a customer to feel defensive and apprehensive. Once these emotions take hold, they will feel less in control of the situation. At this point, they are likely to close up and be reluctant to answer your questions in any comprehensive way. It is, therefore, vital that throughout your questioning, you ensure your customer always has a sense of control. Questions can be prefaced with phrases like these:

- 'I don't know whether you found this, but ...'
- 'I don't know whether this is relevant, but ...'
- 'I'd be interested to understand your feelings or opinions on ...'
- 'Other customers have said ... but I'd be curious to know your thoughts ...'

The implication is that your customer must tell you; they decide. This helps to give them a sense of control. It also prevents asking questions too presumptively. Also, asking customers for their feelings, thoughts and opinions will help them to feel comfortable. People generally like giving their opinion and we have all got into trouble for giving our opinion when it has not been wanted. Asking a customer for their views helps to prevent questioning seeming like a cross examination; which of course, it should never be. Questioning is an opportunity for both you and your customer to learn about their situation and draw the best conclusions available.

The more you can help a customer feel good about being involved in the process, the more likely they are to relax and engage with you. So, if a customer asks a question, responding with the phrase 'That is a good question', before answering, will make them feel positive about getting involved in the process. If a customer makes a good observation, comment; saying: 'That's an interesting point'. If they ask you something you were going to come to later, say, 'I'm glad you asked me that.'

Being involved in the sales process is not easy for a customer. Conveying possibility can introduce new ideas which may suggest change and imply that currently the customer has got it wrong. The whole process can, therefore, be extremely daunting and uncomfortable. A doctor will try to put a nervous patient at ease in order to help them to help their patient. You must put your customer at ease, so they will open up and give you the best chance of helping them. A doctor is in a privileged position. If a doctor abuses their position with a patient, it is malpractice and they can be struck off. Equally, when selling, you are in a privileged position. Therefore, you must have equally high standards of integrity. If you cannot help, you must be fully prepared to walk away.

Always remain open-minded. It might be that customers will raise matters that you have not previously considered and there is always going to be an element of having to think on your feet. One of the many advantages of targeting niche markets, tight geographical areas, companies of certain sizes or a particular demographic is that many of the problems the clients are facing are likely to be similar. This will minimize the amount of times you find yourself being put on the spot. Recent conversations with other customers will provide valuable insights that will be relevant in other meetings.

PART IV: PROBLEMS AND SOLUTIONS ARE NOT ENOUGH

BUYING CRITERIA – THE WIDER CONTEXT

Before prescribing any tablets, our doctor will ask a patient questions regarding their lifestyle. This is because although the doctor's preferred course of tablets may make the patient healthier, quicker; they may also make the patient a little drowsy during the day. If the patient works with dangerous machinery, or something similar which requires concentration, the preferred treatment will be inappropriate. The correct solution, in this case, is for a lesser dosage to be taken only in the evening, albeit over a longer period of time. The doctor has to ensure that the context is fully understood before offering a solution.

When engaging with a customer, there is no point simply understanding the issues, challenges and problems that they have. In order to suggest appropriate solutions, you need to understand their situation properly. This means one has to fully appreciate the context within which these issues, challenges and problems exist.

In order to understand the context of a situation, one must be aware that every buying decision is affected by emotional, practical, personal and professional issues. Without having a real understanding of all these areas, there is a danger that any solutions suggested will seem inappropriate to a customer.

A Problem Map™ provides us with the basis to understand the issues a customer may have. Using a Problem Map™ will give us clarity when questioning about the issues themselves. There will be practical, emotional, personal and professional considerations related directly to the challenges presented in our Problem Map™. However, when questioning, one will not be able to rely solely on our Problem Map™. There will be other areas that one must cover, which will enable understanding in a fuller context.

WHO ELSE IS INVOLVED?

A man walks into a store looking for a satellite navigation system. The sales person, understanding the problems that they can solve, asks pertinent questions of the gentleman. After a thorough discussion, the sales person suggests an appropriate solution. They suggest a solid and reliable system. Although it is not one of the most attractive looking units, it is, however, one of the best. On being presented with the solution, the gentleman hesitates, explains that he needs to think about it and leaves without making a purchase.

Q: What went wrong?
The sales person failed to ask a vital question. They had assumed the satellite navigation system was for the gentleman concerned. Indeed, it was. This was certainly the impression he gave during the discussion. However, the sales person should have asked, 'Will anybody else be using the satellite navigation?'

The sales person would have then discovered that the gentleman lends his car to his teenage daughter at the weekends. He was keen for her to have use of the satellite navigation because he did not like the idea of her getting lost at night whilst driving alone. The unit the sales person suggested was a little bulky and unattractive and he was unsure whether his teenage daughter would be willing to use it. He was looking for something a little slicker and smarter. Therefore, on being presented with the unit, he decided it was not right and to look elsewhere. The sales person, of course, could have helped and did have a model that would have been appropriate. However, by failing to ask who else may be using the item, they did not fully understand the context in which this decision would be made.

When questioning, therefore, it is important not to solely focus on the person or persons to whom you are speaking and forget the broader picture. In order to ensure you look at the bigger picture, you must understand who else will be involved in making the purchasing decision, who will be affected by the decision and who will have use of the product or service being considered.

THE CUSTOMER'S EXPECTATIONS

When looking to make a purchase, a customer will have their own preconceived expectations. Some of these expectations may be of a practical nature, some may fulfil emotional requirements. Sometimes expectations will be unrealistic. At other times they may be easily achievable. These expectations will often form part of the customer's criteria to buy. If one does not reveal what these expectations are, it is possible that opportunities will be lost. Therefore, one must ask questions that will reveal the buyer's criteria. For example:

- 'How will you know when you have this right?'
- 'How do you see it working?'
- 'How would you like this to pan out?'
- 'Let's say that you had this sorted out, could you explain what it would look like?

By asking these types of questions, you will begin to understand your buyer's thought processes and uncover the practical and emotional criteria they have.

BARRIERS TO PURCHASING

There will be other considerations that a buyer will take into account which may prevent a purchase taking place. These barriers may involve the politics within an organization or a relationship, or events and situations that may arise. Without understanding what these obstacles are, you may find they make inappropriate suggestions to your customer, or fail to take into account important factors when offering a solution. It will, therefore, be necessary to ask questions like:

- 'What do you think would prevent this from working?'
- 'What would stop this working?'
- 'Are there any reasons you can foresee that would prevent this from happening?'

Asking these questions will often provide valuable information if you are going to help your customer. So, for example, when you ask the HR director if anyone else is involved in the decision, they will give an honest answer, 'no'. However, later on, when you ask them, 'What do you think may prevent this from working?' after considerable thought, they may reply that the financial director may veto the proposal if they do not feel there will be a proper return on investment. By asking this question, you start to understand the politics of the organization. You become aware of the need to include the financial director in the buying process. You also find out that return on investment is a key buying criteria.

EMOTIONAL CONSIDERATIONS

There are some items that we purchase without much emotion. These will be different depending on the person. So, for example, there will be people buying petrol whose emotions influence their decision. However, many people buy petrol solely based on price and convenience without much emotion. Similarly, when purchasing utilities, such as gas and electricity, many people will buy solely based on price and convenience, with little regard for anything else.

However, most purchases are influenced by our emotions and in a large amount of cases, our emotions are the most important factor in any decision we make. It is vital to understand the emotions your customer has. Therefore, when exploring a customer's circumstances, we must ask them how they feel about a situation as well as the practical aspects of the issue they may have. So, a customer may make a comment on the fact that they cannot track their engineers when they are on the road. By asking how they feel about that, they uncover their emotional concerns and worries that questions regarding the practicality of the situation would not reveal.

OTHER USEFUL QUESTIONS

Ultimately, the only reason for asking questions is to ensure you have a complete understanding of your customer's situation. How many questions and what questions are asked will depend on the individual circumstances of the problem. Interesting areas you might need to consider, depending on the situation, will be:

- How did the problem arise?
- When did it start?
- How long has it been going on?
- Is it being caused by something else?
- Is it causing other issues?
- When did you decide to look for a solution?
- What precipitated that decision?
- How long have you been looking?
- Is this issue ongoing or critical at certain times?
- What are those times?
- What aspects of the business does the problem affect?
- How does it affect those areas?
- Who does it affect?

- Have you ever tried to do anything about it before?
- If so, when?
- What happened?
- Why did it work?/Why didn't it work?
- What has changed since then?

NEVER ASSUME

When you are asking questions, you must clarify everything. This may be obvious if you are unsure whether you understood what your customer said. However, even if you think you do understand, never assume. You must ask questions in order to clarify that you fully comprehend what your customer is saying. For example, your customer may tell you that they had tried to rectify this issue before but it proved too expensive. It is easy to assume you know what 'too expensive' means, but in reality, you do not. It could mean:

- The solution exceeded the figure they had in mind.
- They simply did not have the money and could not afford it.
- They only have sign-off for a certain amount and would have had to introduce their boss into the decision-making process, which they were unwilling to do.

Assuming that we understand what our customer means could result in us completely misconstruing the situation and prevent us from suggesting an appropriate solution. You must, therefore, clarify exactly what your customer is saying. This is best achieved by a comment such as:

> 'I'm sorry. I'm not sure I fully understand. Can I just ask, in what way was it too expensive?'

Apologizing makes the question non-threatening and takes away any feeling that you are questioning the authenticity of what they are saying. You do not want them to feel like they are being challenged, merely, that you are trying to understand. Apologizing, therefore, helps to put your customer at ease. Also, remember that your customer knows what they are talking about; it is your fault that you do not understand.

So, you may be told by a client that they have funding for a project. You must not take this at face value. Instead, you could reply:

- 'I'm sorry, I don't understand. When you say that you have funding, what exactly do you mean?'
- 'I'm sorry, can you just explain that a little bit more for me?'

Because, they could mean:

- They have agreed the funding in principle with the bank, but will still need to get their approval if they decide to go ahead. (In which case, you now know, in order to help them, your solution will also have to satisfy criteria set by the bank)
- They have applied for funding, but are waiting for approval.
- They haven't applied for funding, but know it is available. (In which case, you learn two things:
  I Your buying cycle will now take longer as your customer will be waiting for approval.
  II Your solution will have to fulfil the requirements of the available funding.)

Without clarifying the general answers a customer will give, you cannot hope to fully understand the position they are in.

THE IMPORTANCE OF PARAPHRASING

Even when you clarify everything that your customer has said, it is still possible to misinterpret them or for there to be a miscommunication. Any inaccuracies in your understanding of your customer's situation may render any suggestion you make inappropriate. It is, therefore, useful to paraphrase back to your customer, in order to prevent this from happening. So, you may say:

> *'So let me understand, Sarah, just to make sure that I have it right ...'*

Again always blame yourself. It is not her fault that you are unsure that you understand, but yours:

> *' ... Just to make sure that I have this right; there is funding available. You have not applied for it yet, but you feel that you will qualify for this funding because it is for training and you do fit into the geographical and business sector criteria?'*

If you reiterated correctly, Sarah will confirm this. If you have misunderstood, she will correct you. By taking one step back and repeating what you thought Sarah said, you ensure there is no miscommunication. Not only this, but you will demonstrate your conscientiousness in trying to truly understand her situation. This will have the added advantage of giving your customer confidence in your ability to help them.

ANYTHING ELSE?

'Anything else?' is one of the most important questions you can ask. These two words can uncover a myriad of issues, concerns and requirements. A client will often repeat to you the same surface story they tell everybody. When you ask 'anything else?' you often uncover issues at a deeper level. So, whenever you have finished questioning a customer around a certain area, it is worth asking, 'anything else?' When they have finished responding you can ask again, 'anything else?' People will often tell you what they think you want to hear or what they think, on first analysis, is most important. The question, 'anything else?' will uncover a lot of other information and areas a customer may never have explored otherwise.

Asking the question 'anything else?' will often require your customer to give a situation further consideration. On occasion, they may ask 'have I missed something?' to which you need only to reply, 'I don't know, I am just asking to make sure I have not missed anything.' If you do not ask your customer if there is anything else, you are in danger of missing information that may be important.

LISTENING

Listening is something that most of us do not do particularly well. If you ever watch people interacting in a restaurant, a bar or elsewhere, you will notice them talking over each other all the time. We all like to be listened to and we all have moments in our lives when we feel we are ignored or misunderstood. Therefore, to interact with someone who is truly interested in you and does not interrupt is refreshing. If someone is really listening to us, we will respond favourably because it is unusual. In order to be effective, you must indicate to your customer that you are listening. Ensure you make eye contact if you are in a face to face meeting. By using verbal responses such as, 'I see' or 'Uh huh' you will indicate to a customer that you are interested in what they are saying, which in turn, will help encourage them to talk.

- When you are questioning, you are diagnosing.
- You are in listening mode, not talking mode.

The only talking you should be doing is to ask the next question, clarify a statement, or reiterate the previous point.

Try not to spend too much time thinking about the next question while your customer is talking, because you will miss something important. You will find, with experience, the next question will come to you and the conversation will flow. However, do not worry if there is a little silence while you think of the next question to ask. Your customer will often appreciate this because it means that you are really listening and taking on board what they are saying. Your attentiveness will give them more confidence in your suggested solutions later on in the process. Moreover, you will often find that in order to fill a silence, your customer will say something else that would have otherwise been left unsaid. This information can often prove extremely important.

Listening properly means:

- Hearing.
- Understanding.
- Remembering.

In order to ensure we hear exactly what our customer says, we must concentrate and pay attention. To ensure you understand, you must ask clarifying questions and paraphrase back to your customer. Finally, in order to remember, you must take notes. Write everything down. Without notes, you will not be able to recall the conversation properly and it will be something that you forget that proves to be vital. Listen to both what is said and what is not said. Sometimes, what a customer does not say can be just as important as what they do say.

Ultimately, you must ensure that you ask **all** the appropriate questions. This is the diagnosis. If you get the diagnosis wrong, the solution will be wrong. Selling is not only about problems and solutions. Unless you truly understand the full context of your buyer's situation, you will not be in a position to suggest appropriate solutions.

When It's Time to Talk

13

If a doctor misses something important when carrying out a diagnosis, then the patient can ultimately be prescribed the wrong medication.

The same is true in a sales meeting. If you miss something when speaking to your potential customer, there is every chance that you will suggest the wrong solution.

Therefore, you must never start talking before you are sure you really understand your customer's situation. A doctor does not need to say much during a consultation beyond asking questions. It may only be in the latter part, when the doctor gives a diagnosis and makes some suggestions, that he or she really starts to talk.

Similarly, apart from asking questions, initially, you should say very little else. Success is not dependent on how much you say. The focus of the meeting should be on your customer. As no-one can know their situation better than they do, it is your customer who should be talking.

When selling, people say too much, because they are too concerned with their own agenda; that is, doing the deal. Do not worry about the transaction at all. When visiting your doctor, their first concern is not what type of tablets can be prescribed, or what injection to give, or to which specialist you can be referred. The conclusion of the visit, at that moment, is irrelevant. What is of real concern to the doctor is getting the diagnosis correct, because the ramifications of getting the diagnosis wrong are, potentially, very severe. Conversely, a solution suggested by the doctor, after a thorough diagnosis, is much more likely to be accepted by the patient.

It is no different in a sales meeting. If you get the diagnosis wrong, the ramifications are severe. It could either mean taking on inappropriate work and letting a customer down, or alternatively missing out on an opportunity when you could have helped.

It is therefore, only time to talk when you are satisfied that you have completed your diagnosis, you have asked all the relevant questions and, as a result, you think you have a good understanding of your customer's situation. Of course, however thorough you are, as you enter into a discussion with your customer, new information may come to light. When this happens, if necessary, you may have to go back into diagnosis mode and ask some further questions.

ADDING VALUE

Once you open your mouth, you are conveying possibility – exploring options and ideas in order to help your customer. To be effective, you must have a good understanding of the possibilities available and their application. That means being an expert in your field.

Demonstrating your expertise to your customer should not be done for its own sake but in order to add value. When discussing a customer's issues and situation you should try and provide some ideas, tips or information that they would not know about otherwise. This is true in all selling situations. However, it is especially pertinent when selling services. When selling a service, because it cannot be seen or touched, the only aspect the customer can buy is the person sitting in front of them. Therefore, giving value demonstrates expertise and builds confidence and trust with your customer.

Once you give a customer a useful idea or tip, or some information, you are no longer perceived as a sales person, but as an expert. The expertise that you demonstrate will help solidify the relationship and take some risk out of the purchase in your customer's eyes. By adding value, a customer will recognize that you really understand your subject. This will help them feel comfortable and make them more inclined to buy from you.

Do not be scared that you are giving too much information away. There may be the odd prospect who will try to learn as much from you as possible, in order to try and undertake the activity themselves. However, these people are rare and a cynical outlook will mean missing out on opportunities. You are not required to tell people everything you know; in a one or two hour meeting, this should not be possible in any case. You may hold some ideas back; however, being overly cautious may prevent you from adding the value that would have encouraged your customer to buy.

WORKING WITH YOUR CUSTOMER

When it is time to talk, you will use your expertise to explore options, ideas and possibilities. Understanding that you do this **with** your customer is of vital importance. You do it together. This is one of the fundamental aspects people get wrong. So many sellers sell **at** their client. Even after questioning properly, they will then take out their Power-Point and revert to presentation mode. This is not the way to do it.

Conveying possibility is often difficult because, inadvertently, the implication can be that what your customer is currently doing is wrong. Therefore, the way a customer comes to this realization will affect how it is received. You cannot expect your customer to sit passively while you tell them how it is. Even after a thorough diagnosis, customers can still feel they are losing control of the process and become very defensive.

Reverting to selling **at** a customer, even after engaging them with questions, can still result in an adversarial situation. Telling them what they should be doing and giving them the benefit of your wisdom may not go down well. Doing something different is scary and once you start telling a customer what is good for them, even with the best of intentions, they will often be looking for the catch.

Never forget that a selling situation can be extremely uncomfortable for a customer and they will throw up objections to justify the status quo, rather than having to face change. Therefore, the way that you deliver your suggestions may determine whether a constructive conversation occurs.

Selling is about helping people. You need to become partners and work at solving your customer's issues and problems together. You should be selling **with** your customer, not **at** them. The key to doing this is to ensure they are empowered at all times. This means involving your customer in the process. Ask their opinion:

- 'What do you think of this …?'
- 'I don't know if this is right, but let me make a suggestion …'
- 'We could do …; what are your thoughts?'

By taking this approach, your customer is no longer looking for the catch, but instead, is working out a solution together with you. Ultimately, it is not your solution anyway; it is theirs. They may not buy what you suggest, but are likely to buy what they suggest. In other words, you must allow your customer to take ownership of the solution.

The language that you use with a customer is vitally important. When referring to an issue or a solution, refer to 'we' and not 'you'. For example, you might say:

- 'One of the options **we** have', rather than, 'One of the options **you** have.'
- 'The situation **we** have here', rather than, 'The situation **you** have here.'

Referring to 'we' rather than 'you' is the language of a partnership. Metaphorically, you are no longer sitting on opposite sides of the table, but are sitting beside each other in order to find the best solution.

MAKING YOUR SUGGESTIONS

Before making your suggestions, it is worth reminding your customer of the problem first. So, for example, instead of saying, 'One of the things that we could do is …' you may say, 'I know you said that you are struggling to find a suitable candidate. One of the things that we can do is …'

In this way, you remind them of the issue before suggesting the solution. This is because you need to ensure the customer understands your thought processes. You are taking them on a journey and, therefore, you must ensure that you both start at the same place. Do not rely on them remembering an issue that they mentioned previously in the conversation.

It is sometimes worth introducing your suggestions by citing other examples of customers who you have helped previously. Referring to a past customer enables you to introduce a new idea in a non-threatening way. By using a relevant example, you can demonstrate a real understanding of their situation. Finally, talking about others, who you have managed to help, provides reassurance, as you establish successes from the past.

TELLING YOUR STORY/DEVELOPING A NARRATIVE

When it is time to talk, the customer will obviously want to know something about you and your company. The context in which this information is disclosed will be of vital importance. The fact that you may have been trading for ten years, in itself, may not be that significant. However, imparting this information, in a subtle way, may be essential in that it will give people confidence that you are a solid organization. Also, the implication is that to survive for ten years, you must be doing something right.

There will be aspects of your product or service which will be important to communicate, for they will highlight reasons as to why you are in a good position to solve the particular issues a customer may have. The way this information is conveyed may have a dramatic effect on how successful a meeting is.

- There are no features and there are no benefits.
- There are only problems and solutions; together with the agenda and buying criteria of your customer.

Therefore, you should only talk about what is relevant to your customer. Entering into lengthy presentations about your business, your product or service and the general advantages you offer, will be irrelevant to a customer and they will stop listening. Many people have a ready-prepared PowerPoint presentation, or something equivalent, which they give in the meeting. However, this will inevitably mean introducing aspects of your product or service that are of no concern to the customer, their situation and the challenges they face. For example, showing your slide on 'why you can deliver at a speed unrivalled by competitors' is ridiculous, if speed of delivery is inconsequential to the customer with whom you are talking. Equally, skipping through slides that you realize are irrelevant looks shoddy.

By taking this approach, you start to move away from being an expert and a partner and revert back to positioning yourself as a sales person. Talking about everything will overwhelm a customer and can actually lead to paralysis. In other words, they will be so overwhelmed that they may feel that they are not in a position to make a decision. Therefore, you should only say enough in order to establish credibility, prove competence and help solve the issues that they have.

Different customers will require different degrees of information before they feel able to reach a decision. However, whoever the customer is, information must be imparted as part of a narrative; that is, a way of explaining your product or service, where everything is linked to the solution. Within this context, you create an environment where other information can be given seamlessly, such as your years of experience and how you work. Rather than having a ready-made presentation, it is better to have a narrative which can be altered depending on your situation. This narrative does not have to be given as a presentation, but can be worked into your conversation.

In order to cultivate your story, you need to take a central theme and develop the solutions, the way you work, and other relevant details around it. The theme may be based on why the company was started, a particular system or product that has been developed, or how the company evolved, etc. Whatever theme you choose, developing your narrative in this way will allow you to create a story. The story must always be centred on solutions that will be of interest to your customer. The purpose of the narrative is to give your customer a context, in order to provide a more substantial sense of your offering.

For example, if you were to use 'why the company was started' as your theme for a solution-focused narrative, you would not say:

> '*I started the company five years ago in my house. We grew quite quickly and moved into offices six months later when I took on my first member of staff …*'

This is irrelevant to your customer and not solution based at all. However, you may use this theme to say:

> '*I started the company five years ago to help businesses with their high level communications. We therefore only concentrate on business-to-business, which I know is your area of concern. Focusing on business-to-business means we ensure that everything is closely monitored …*'

This second example is the beginning of a narrative which will only focus on relevant information to the requirements of your customer.

Your story can be changed or moulded to the situation in which you find yourself. However, there will be core elements around which your story can be built. These will be the key deliverables of your product or service, which will, therefore, be relevant to all customers. For example, you may only work in Wales. Therefore, this is core to your service delivery. If this is not relevant to the customer, then you are not going to be able to help them.

People relate to stories, enjoy them and are likely to retain more of the information you impart in this way. Moreover, stories tend to give a customer the feeling that they have a real understanding of who you are. The more familiar they feel with you, the more comfortable they will be in using your product or service.

PROVIDING REASSURANCE BY UNDERSTANDING RISK

All prospective customers have a fear of failure, which can become a barrier to making a purchase. Some of their concerns may be specific to the product or service you are selling. There will be anxieties based on whether the product or service will deliver and the resulting issues which may be caused by the purchase. For example:

> A customer may be convinced that a software package will deliver the required results, but may worry about the culture change and training of staff that implementation will require. In this scenario, just selling the software by addressing the problem it solves is not enough. Without being able to help with the subsequent issues, the risk of implementation becomes too high. Therefore, it is unlikely that any deal will occur.

Other concerns may be based around price, the opinion of other people and the fear of change itself. Before addressing any customers, you must have a good understanding of the risks they perceive they are taking with regard to your product or service. When in dialogue with your customer, you must build in as many assurances as possible. This may involve a price match, if they find it cheaper elsewhere, a money back guarantee or some sort of initial trial period.

It is unlikely that you will be able to take all the risk out of a purchase. You must give as much reassurance as possible, but be honest with a customer if they highlight risks that you cannot negate. Ultimately, there will be a straight choice between them keeping the problem or trying a solution.

A doctor may prescribe tablets with some mild side effects. However, the side effects should be minimal compared with the illness that needs curing.

Similarly, as long as you can keep the risk relatively low, in comparison with the value the solution provides, there will be customers willing to buy. However, the more risk you can eradicate, the easier the buying decision becomes.

EXPLAIN EVERYTHING

Finally, make sure that you explain everything. Do not assume that people understand and know what you are talking about. Sometimes, when you are living with solutions everyday, you start to devalue what you know. If you do not explain something to a customer, it may become a barrier later on. They may not purchase because they do not understand why a solution has been suggested or how it will work. Worse still, if they do purchase, you may not meet their expectations based on a miscommunication because of something left unexplained.

If you are worried that you may be telling people about matters that they already know, then start your explanation by stating exactly this:

> *'I apologize if you already know this, but let me just explain ...'*

In this way, you put people at ease. If you are then telling someone something they did not know, they do not need to feel uncomfortable, because at no time do they have to admit to not knowing. On the other hand, if it is something of which they are already aware, by apologizing in advance, you are neither patronizing nor insulting them.

Objections and Concerns

14

When selling, people often fail to distinguish between objections and concerns.

A concern comes from a customer who feels involved in the sales process. They are in partnership and working with us towards a solution. The fears or worries that they raise are in relation to how the purchase will affect them. This is because they see themselves as a potential buyer. Therefore, concerns are buying signals. They are not being raised to catch us out, but because the buyer is predisposed to making the purchase. When one is faced with a concern, it is as part of a continuing discussion, in working towards an acceptable solution. For example:

> You go and see your doctor who you have been visiting over the past twenty years. Because of your previous experiences, you trust them and are predisposed to acting on their suggestions. Your doctor recommends a particular course of medication. At this point you raise a genuine concern; you have a challenging week ahead and cannot afford to take medication which will cause you to be drowsy. You only raise this concern because you fully intend to heed your doctor's advice if an acceptable solution can be found.

In this scenario, the doctor may have an alternative solution. They may, however, only have the medication that will make you drowsy. Maybe the medication can be delayed for a week; on the other hand, that might lead to some very severe complications.

It is important that you understand the concerns customers are likely to have with your own product or service. These may relate to the knock-on effects a solution may cause and the risks involved in purchasing. The more creative you can be, the more probable it is that you will find an acceptable solution and eradicate your customer's concerns. However, there will not always be an ideal solution available and compromises may have to be sought. You must prepare for this by understanding what the pay-offs are in relation to your own product or service.

UNDERSTANDING OBJECTIONS

Unlike concerns, an objection comes from someone who is not pre-disposed, at that time, to using your product or service. They will have a dislike or reluctance towards your offering, as they understand it. An objection is raised as a barrier to a purchase being made.

It is possible, that the same issue can be a concern with one customer and an objection with another. It will be the context, words used and body language that will indicate what you are facing. For example, a customer may have a problem with your delivery times. This could be expressed either as an objection or a concern.

> *Concern: 'I was really hoping to take delivery twice a week.'*

> *Objection: 'I want a delivery twice a week and you only offer once a week.'*

Many training courses and books on selling perpetuate the myth that objections are good. We are told they are buying signals and that we should welcome them, because this is where the selling really starts.

The reality is, the opposite is true. *Objections are not good.*

When we are faced with objections, we do not feel good about them. They make things difficult and can make us feel uncomfortable. These feelings are natural and are not wrong. For years people in selling have been told to welcome objections. We do not want to hear them and we do not welcome them. In reality, if you face a lot of objections, you are unlikely to get a sale. People do not necessarily believe what you say, but they normally believe what they say. Therefore, every time your customer has an objection, it reinforces in their own mind why the solution is not right and why they should not make a purchase. Every time they repeat this, they are one step closer to convincing themselves that your offer is wrong.

Also, the more objections you receive, the more the sales process will become adversarial. However convivial you are, it is very difficult for the process not to start resembling a boxing match, wherein you are thrown an objection, by your customer, and you retaliate with an answer. Needless to say, this is not a conducive environment to helping someone and solving their problems.

PREVENTING OBJECTIONS

It may appear that we have painted a very bleak picture, for if we face too many objections, it may seem like the sales process is doomed to fail. Indeed, this is the case. However, we can minimize the objections we receive.

Imagine you want to buy a new computer and you are recounting this to a friend. Would they ask you what objections you have? Of course not. You may have requirements, e.g. you want it to be light, so it is easy to carry. You may even have concerns based on previous experiences, so you may be looking for something that is durable, because your last laptop was damaged when it was dropped on the floor.

However, before entering into a buying process, you will have no objections.

> Q: *If you do not have any objections before you enter into a*
> *buying process, from where do objections come?*
> A: *Sales people.*

Objections come from the sales person. If you have not diagnosed properly and do not have a full understanding of your customer's situation, you may make an inappropriate suggestion or comment. An objection is a response to inappropriate remarks made by the seller. This highlights another difference between an objection and a concern.

Concerns are raised during the course of a frank and honest discussion between buyer and seller and do not necessarily relate to anything a seller has said. In other words, they may be a part of the buying criteria and agenda your customer already has. Objections, on the other hand, are direct responses to inappropriate statements made by the seller. For example:

Without a full understanding of your customer's situation, you suggest delivering your goods on a Friday. This is a completely inappropriate day for your customer and results in an immediate objection. Friday is not the only day you can deliver, although it was convenient. By asking your customer when they were hoping to take delivery, the objection could have been prevented.

Put simply, the best way to handle objections is not to create any.

Sellers create objections because they make comments which have no relevance, or offer solutions which are unsuitable, impractical, or inappropriate. If you undertake a proper diagnosis and refrain from speaking before this has been achieved, you are unlikely to say the wrong thing and create objections. Moreover, if you are unsure of an aspect of your customer's situation, ask and qualify before suggesting anything. In this way you will not have to deal with objections, because none will be created.

PRE-HANDLING OBJECTIONS

It is very unlikely that any solution you can offer is a perfect one. There-fore, there may be a few objections that you find arise on a regular basis. You will learn what these are from interactions that you have with customers. You may also be able to pre-empt some objections by understanding where your offering is different from your competition and, therefore, what expectations customers may have. Looking at your Problem Map™ and thinking through the risks inherent in a purchase may also help in understanding objections that you might receive.

As you gain experience of selling a particular product or service, you will know what objections you frequently encounter. It is likely that there will only ever be a few. When you know what these are, the idea is to pre-handle them. By pre-handle, we mean that you introduce them, rather than waiting for your customer to raise them in response to something you have said. For example:

> You may offer an inexpensive solution where everything is dealt with online. In order to keep costs down, you do not give customers an opportunity to see a company representative once they have entered into an agreement.

You may know that your solution is commercially viable for certain types of customers. However, your solution may be unusual in the market place where customers are used to meeting on a regular basis. If this is an objection you find you are confronting regularly, then you can pre-handle it as part of your narrative. So you may say:

> 'Many of our customers have been worried that everything is managed online. Actually, our research shows that only 3% of customers ever request a face-to-face meeting. However, in order to deliver this, we would have to charge 10% more for the service, and we would rather pass these savings onto our customers. What our customers have found is that because we regularly update our frequently asked questions page, and because we have support staff on the other end of a computer, 24/7, they always get an instant response and it is actually often a better experience than being restricted to seeing someone during office hours.'

So always pre-handle the few objections you know people may have about your product or service. It is important to continuously learn from the interactions you have with customers. If there are particular objections that occur on a regular basis, you must ensure that you understand why. Either:

- You are creating the objection unnecessarily and must, therefore, prevent this from happening.
- As the market evolves, you need to alter your product or service for the solution to remain compelling.
- It is one of a few objections you receive regularly and, therefore, needs to be pre-handled, in the future, as part of your narrative.

MANAGING OBJECTIONS

We know that objections are not good. Therefore, in an ideal world, we would never get any. By not creating objections and pre-handling the few we understand may arise, we can minimize the occasions when objections will occur. However, inevitably, there will be times when we are confronted by objections. When this happens, we manage the objection by doing three things.

1   Acknowledge the objection:
    On receiving an objection, the first thing you must do is acknowledge it. If you come across as dismissive in any way, you will not be able to take your customer with you when answering the objection they have. For why should they listen to you if you have seemingly disregarded their thoughts? You are not required to agree, but, by demonstrating recognition of what they have said with a simple, 'I see' or 'I understand,' you show your customer that you are listening and value their point of view.

2   Understand the objection:
    It is impossible to manage an objection that you do not understand. If you try and answer an objection without a proper comprehension of the issue, you will make matters worse. For example, a potential customer says:

    'I am not happy that your company only delivers once a week.'

    Many people will assume they understand the problem and will immediately try to justify the reasons why delivery only happens on a weekly basis. The reality is, you do not understand the objection properly at this juncture, for the customer could mean several things. Do they mean:
    - Their previous supplier always delivered twice a week. In actuality, there is no particular reason why this needs to happen, but has become habit and, therefore, part of their expectation?
    - They have insufficient room in the warehouse to take only one larger delivery on a weekly basis?

- They employ someone twice weekly to meet the deliveries and do not want to reduce their hours because they like them and know they are in need of the money?

So, when faced with this objection, rather than answer straight away, you must clarify the situation. So you might say:

- 'I understand, please can you explain that a little more?'
- 'I see, please can you explain why delivery once a week is not acceptable?

If you find they have insufficient room in the warehouse, explaining efficiencies and cost savings as your reason for only delivering weekly would be irrelevant. It would not solve the problem. So always ensure you clarify any objection before you attempt to reply. If you are told you are too expensive, you can respond with:

'I see, I do apologize, but I am not sure I fully understand. Please would you just explain what you mean by too expensive?'

If they say they must have it in green, you could respond with:

'I understand; please would you explain your reason for wanting green?'

3   Answer the objection:

Once you fully understand the objection, there will be two scenarios:

I   You actually cannot help them at all. For example, your customer requires your product in green. Their reasoning is absolutely compelling. Unfortunately, you do not produce the item in green and it will not be cost effective to do so. In this scenario, your best outcome is to be able to recommend the customer to someone who may be able to help. Obviously this is an outcome you do not want to happen on too many occasions. If it does, there are two possibilities. Either you are targeting the wrong people, or your solution is not commercially viable. For example, maybe you should start producing the item in green.

II   You can help your customer.

Helping your customer may be simple. They explain they want a delivery twice a week and when you understand why, it makes sense. You can accommodate them, so agree.

Sometimes, however, it is not that simple. Although you can help, it will require a shift in your customer's thinking. They may want the item in green and you only produce it in black. On hearing their explanation, your experience tells you that black would be a better colour for them. How you manage this situation, though, will be vital to the final outcome. Telling a customer they are wrong and explaining why, is likely to lead to an adversarial situation. You may also, inadvertently, leave a customer feeling stupid. Although everything you say may be entirely correct, you will not produce an environment conducive for a purchase to happen. Therefore, you may win the argument but lose the customer.

The principle to managing this situation is to show empathy by giving examples of other satisfied customers who have had the same concerns. Only then, do you introduce the alternative solution. This approach allows you to explain new concepts and ideas in a non-threatening way. So, your reply to the customer who wanted the item in green may be:

> *'I see; it is interesting, we have worked with many customers who have said the same thing. They wanted it in green for the exact reason that you've given, but actually what they found was, that by using the black version ...' and then you go on to explain the solution.*

By referring to other users, you are showing empathy and demonstrating that you really understand their thinking as you have had other customers with the same problem. Far from implying that they are stupid, you are actually suggesting that they are in good company as other customers have said the same. Finally, you introduce a new idea in a non-adversarial and non-threatening way.

USING TESTIMONIALS

Regardless of whether a customer has concerns or objections, they will not be ready to buy until any worries, fears or other issues causing reluctance are eased. We have already demonstrated the important use of empathy when answering objections. This is achieved by citing previous customer experiences. There is no more powerful way to do this than having testimonials to show your customer. Having previous and existing customers advocating your product or service is very powerful and reassuring to a prospective buyer.

These testimonials may be written and presented in hard copy or could be stored on your laptop in electronic form. Alternatively you may even have short video clips of customer testimonials. Some customers may offer to write or record a testimonial for you, others may even write something without being prompted. When a customer mentions you have done a really good job, you should ask them if they would write or if you could record a testimonial. Other customers may be happy for you to pass their details on to a prospective buyer for them to use as a reference. Again, this will be very powerful and will help to allay any concerns or objections a buyer may have.

Finally, by making sure that you are on your customer's side and putting their interests first, you position yourself as a partner, trying to help, rather than making the sales process an adversarial one. This positioning helps to minimize the objections one receives and allows them to be managed effectively. In this way, objections are rarely a barrier to a sale.

Traditionally It's Called Closing

The term 'closing' has traditionally been used to describe the part of the sales process when the transaction is agreed. 'Closing a sale' has been used as a phrase meaning, getting the deal.

'Closing' is a terrible word to employ and comes directly from the traditional transactional approach to selling. If we perceive sales as all about the transaction, then deals are, indeed, closed. 'Closing' implies, the end of something; the finish. If selling is only about the transaction, then once the deal is agreed, the process has come to an end.

Sales Therapy® does not look at selling in this way. The most valuable asset created during the sales process is the relationship. A sale is, therefore, never closed and never ended. If our relationship with a customer is mutually beneficial, why should it end? We want it to continue for a long time. In fact, in the commercial environment in which we find ourselves today, retaining customers and, therefore, developing relationships, is an absolute imperative.

When a customer first agrees to buy, far from being the end, or the 'close', this is often, in fact, merely the beginning.

COMMITMENT; NOT CLOSING

A sale is never closed because an agreement to buy should not be the end. Therefore, it is more helpful to think in terms of commitment. A sale, from the very first engagement with a customer, is developed through a series of commitments. These commitments are made by both parties throughout. For example:

- A phone call may lead to a meeting, whereby a customer commits to give time to seeing you and you commit to be there.
- That meeting may lead to a commitment to trial your product.
- The trial may lead to a commitment to buy.
- As a result of you delivering on your commitments, upgrades and further purchases are made as the relationship continues.

CLOSING MYTHS

There is an irony around the idea of 'closing'. For a sales person or business to be successful, they have to 'close' a certain amount of deals. Therefore, most people in sales are judged by how many deals they get. However, the amount of deals they 'close' has nothing to do with what is traditionally seen as the closing part of the meeting or process. This obsession has led to an embarrassment of nonsense written and spoken about 'closing' over the years.

People will make comments such as, 'He is a good salesman, although he struggles with closing'. Statements such as these are absurd. 'Closing' is not about the last part of a meeting at all but is in fact a result of everything that comes before it. Therefore, by definition, someone who struggles to get deals is not a good sales person.

However, this focus on 'closing' has led to a whole industry dedicating itself to skills which are all but useless. Entire books and courses address techniques such as: 'the assumptive close', 'the alternative close' or 'the puppy dog close'. These methods defy logic. People do not buy because you ask them in a sophisticated way:

> If you do not want the pens, and a sales person asks whether you want the pens in red or green; you will still not want the pens. You will not be bamboozled by the 'alternative close' into buying. And, even if you were, when 2000 cartons of red pens that you do not want arrive at your office, you would not smile sweetly thinking, gosh, that guy was good! More likely, you would refuse to accept the order and write a letter of cancellation.

There are yet more falsehoods that pervade the world of 'closing'. The perceived wisdom is that to obtain the customer's business, you will not ask for the order once, but be required to ask many times. Again, this is ridiculous. If I do not want something, it does not matter how many times you ask. My desire for your product or service does not increase because you ask me 30 times. I will still not want it. In fact, continually asking for the order, when a customer is not ready to buy, is completely counter productive.

Persistently appealing for the customer's business when they are not ready to buy is again borne out of the transactional sales model. There is no better illustration to a customer that the transaction is more important than anything else. Repeated requests for the deal make it clear that the sales person's agenda is their paramount concern. They are, therefore, the sales people we all dislike, the ones with '£' signs in their eyes, who have little regard for the interests of their customer.

This approach will make the sales experience uncomfortable for your customer. Rather than increasing the likelihood of a purchase being made, the environment will not be conducive to allowing someone to buy. We all try to avoid uncomfortable situations if we can, and your customer is no different. Therefore, it is likely that persistently asking for the order will reduce the amount of time you get to spend with your customer, as they will try and end the meeting as soon as possible. By reducing your time together, continually asking for the order minimizes the opportunity of developing the relationship.

Using the 'limited period close', whereby the urgency of making the decision is used as a tool to get the deal, will also damage the relationship. In this scenario, you tell your customer that the special price or offer is only available today. While an offer like this may work in a direct mail piece, or on a website, when you are interacting with someone on a personal level, it creates a high pressure environment.

There may be times when there is good reason for a limited offer, such as a stock clearance, or a deadline that has to be met, e.g. a publishing deadline. However, in these situations, the 'time-limited offer' is a matter of fact, rather than a ruse in order to get someone to agree to buy. Using high pressure techniques to close a deal will come across as sharp practice if there is no compelling reason to do so. Of course, it is possible to invent a compelling reason. However, this demonstrates a complete lack of integrity and is not a helpful approach when trying to build positive relationships. Also, by doing this, you create an 'all or nothing' scenario. For, if the customer believes the deadline exits, they may be coerced into making a purchase. However, if they call the sales person's bluff, they may lose the sale and certainly could lose credibility. For example:

> A sales person for a design agency tells their potential customer they need a decision today in order to schedule the work to be completed within the month. If the customer curtails, the sales person has their order. However, the customer may state that they need to speak to their partner in a couple of days, before a decision can be taken. Once the customer makes this statement, there are three possible scenarios, none of which are great for the sales person.
>
> 1   The sales person sticks to the invented deadline and says the work will not be able to be completed within the month. The customer does not seem to mind, but the sales person has now inadvertently delayed the work by several weeks and possibly the decision, as there is now no urgency at all.

2   The sales person sticks to the invented deadline and says the work will not be able to be completed within the month. The customer needs the work completed within this period and goes elsewhere.

3   The sales person backs down and states that they can manage to fit within the time scales as long as they know within the next few days. Even if the sales person handles this extremely well, they will still lose credibility with the customer and, therefore, some reputation will be lost, having piled on the pressure a few minutes earlier. It is also likely that a customer will ignore any future deadlines the sales person suggests.

In any case, with the amount of choice we have in the market place today, putting unnecessary pressure on a customer will be counter productive. We are all sophisticated buyers. If you tell a customer the price is going up tomorrow, without offering a good explanation, they will see straight through you. It is likely, in this scenario, that they will walk away, if they can, and go elsewhere. Moreover, even if they do purchase, having found the experience less than enjoyable, it is unlikely they will ever recommend you to others or come back again.

WINNING BUSINESS

You do not win business by using clever or high pressure techniques. Neither is constantly asking for the deal effective. In fact, it is not something that is annexed to the end of the meeting at all.

Everything you say and do; every e-mail, every phone call, every text message, every interaction between you and your customer, will influence the final outcome. Everything, from the first contact made, will affect their decision and whether they wish to go ahead. If you:

- target the right people and undertake a thorough diagnosis;
- demonstrate your expertise and gain the person's trust;

- act in your customer's interest and introduce them to relevant solutions;
- take into account their personal, professional, emotional and practical agenda; and
- alleviate some of their fears and the risks of purchase;

then you may well win the business.

This has nothing to do with 'closing' techniques and everything to do with developing relationships and helping customers. If you have a thorough discussion with your customer and you cannot help, then you must be prepared to walk away from the deal. If possible, you should recommend them to someone else. However, if you think you can help, there is no reason why you should not.

You are there to facilitate the process. Ultimately the buyer has the problems, their own purchasing criteria and their various agendas. There is no room for you to bully or trick a customer into making a favourable decision. Even if you get the deal in this way, it is very likely to lead to a difficult customer and a sour relationship. Ultimately, purchasers will make decisions for themselves. Your job is to convey possibility and solve problems, while taking into account all the various agendas and the context within which the buyer is operating. If you undertake this task properly you will find that customers often close themselves.

A doctor does not ask if you want the tablets in red or green. Nor, during a consultation, will they attempt to persuade you to have an injection with the promise of another one free. A good doctor does a thorough diagnosis and then makes honest suggestions. If you are satisfied that the doctor has undertaken the diagnosis properly and has a real understanding of your situation, you will readily pick up the prescription they recommend and take the medication. It is only if you are dissatisfied with their diagnosis, or if you are uncertain that they are acting in your interest, that you will you seek a second opinion. Similarly, like the doctor, all you have to do is make suggestions. No clever techniques; just suggestions.

COMMITMENT COMES IN SMALL STEPS

We are in the business of developing relationships. As long as these are mutually beneficial, we never want them to end. Sales are, therefore, never 'closed'. Instead, the sales process is made up of a series of commitments. A commitment requires action by both parties. For example:

- An agreement to a meeting.
- An agreement to a trial.
- An agreement to a purchase.

After a good meeting with a potential buyer, they may well ask for a proposal. In itself this requires no commitment from them, only work for you. Therefore, when agreeing to send a proposal, also agree a date and time when you can either meet or call to discuss it. No one-sided relationship, in any situation, is a healthy one. As long as both parties are making commitments, the relationship is not one-sided and the process keeps a degree of momentum.

If you undertake a thorough diagnosis, gain a real understanding of your customer's situation and are truly working in partnership with them to obtain the most appropriate solutions; you will experience customers who frequently introduce the idea of the next commitment. In other words, by not focusing on the transaction, but by working hard for your customer, you will often find that no 'closing' will be necessary.

It is unlikely that your customer will be aware of the next stage in the process. It is, therefore, improbable that they will suggest a meeting, or product trial or other appropriate next step. Instead they will ask a question such as, 'What do we do next?' or 'Where do we go from here?' These questions are tantamount to a customer committing themselves to the next phase. For once we have received this question, it is likely that any sensible response will be greeted positively and the sale can move forward.

MAKING SUGGESTIONS

There will be times when it is up to you to move the sale forward. For many customers, a purchase means taking a risk and/or doing something differently. This can be somewhat daunting. Apart from all this, customers will rarely know what the appropriate 'next step' is. They will often need a friendly hand to reassure them and guide them through the process. In other words, you must make it as easy for them to buy as possible.

There are no clever techniques required to move the process forward. All you have to do is make suggestions. For example:

> *'Can I suggest that we make a date to meet?'*

> *'What I would normally suggest, in this situation, is that you trial the system for a month and see how you get on.'*

> *'What I suggest, is that you order 50 initially and then we can go from there.'* Or

> *'What I suggest, is that I undertake an initial six days work with you and then we can see where we are.'*

If you are not sure of an appropriate suggestion to make, and feel it is time to move forward, you can ask them:

> *'What do you think we should do next?'* Or

> *'Where shall we go from here?'*

When answering, your customer will often make a commitment themselves. If they do not, you can then suggest an appropriate 'next step'. For example, they may say:

> *'At this stage I would need to discuss all this with my partner.'*

Your response might be:

> *'I understand; can I suggest we arrange a time for all of us to get together?'*

UNDERSTANDING BUYING SIGNALS

There will be an optimum time, in a conversation, to make appropriate suggestions in order to move the sales process forward. The timing will vary depending on the customer. The customer will indicate to you if this moment arrives by giving you buying signals. Because there are fears and risks involved in making a purchase, buying signals may be the strongest indicator you receive from a customer that they are willing to move forward. If you miss these buying signals, and, therefore, do not make suggestions at the right time, you may lose the opportunity by over-selling.

Over-selling is when you say too much. It is when you introduce too many ideas into a conversation and your customer moves from being ready to make the next commitment to feeling unsure. In other words, your customer's mood changes from one of excitement to one of being overwhelmed. Over-selling will normally lead to a customer feeling they need more time to think about the purchase. It is, therefore, important not to overcomplicate matters and to make suggestions when your customer is giving you buying signals.

Different customers will communicate buying signals in a variety of ways. They might ask:

- how they can pay;
- when you can deliver or about other time scales; or
- what will happen next.

These are all strong buying signals. Alternatively, other strong buying signals would be for a customer to start stating preferences. For example:

'*We would like it in this size …*'

'*We would need it in this colour …*' Or

'*We would need delivery on a Friday …*'

Other buying signals may be more subtle. These may involve a customer getting excited, which you would notice by way of their voice tone or demeanour changing, or by them becoming more engaged in the process.

AGREEING COMMITMENT

Once you have made a suggestion and a commitment has been made, it is important to summarize the prevalent aspects of the agreement.

> 'So, just to confirm, we will send an invoice out on Monday and the goods will be dispatched on Thursday. You should expect to receive them during the early part of the following week …'

It is important that you summarize the main aspects of an agreement. Firstly, it is very reassuring for your customer. Secondly, it ensures that all parties are clear on what has been agreed. It allows for any discrepancies to be sorted out immediately. In the process of a deal being arranged, aspects can become confused. However, a letter confirming wrong details a few days after a meeting can result in a loss of confidence and cancellation before a trading relationship even starts. Summarizing the deal at the time a commitment is being made can prevent problems occurring later down the line.

Following Up – Continuing the Relationship

16

We define selling as conveying possibility and solving problems. Ultimately, it is about helping people. In this way, it is win–win. By helping others, you also help yourself. You will only be in a position to help others by developing relationships. Relationships are not cultivated in a single phone call, a single letter, a single meeting or even on a one-off purchase. They grow over time and with effort.

Whether it is with friends, family or a spouse, we have to work at relationships in order for them to prosper. This is no different in business. Relationships do not just happen; you have to work at them. Continually following up with potential clients, existing clients and lapsed clients is an essential part of the sales process.

At the beginning of this process, it is important to follow up with a customer, by creating the opportunity for a number of touch points. By touch points, we mean contacts that we have with someone. The more familiar a person is with you, the more comfortable they are likely to be. The more comfortable they are, the greater the possibility that some of the risk of the purchase dissipates. This makes it more probable that someone will buy.

For example, below is a sales process where there are five touch points:

1   A telephone call, where a meeting is arranged.
2   A meeting where it is agreed a proposal will be sent and a follow-up call made.
3   The proposal is sent.
4   On the follow-up call, a second meeting is arranged.
5   At the second meeting, a decision whether to purchase is made.

Following the same generic process, we could, however, maximize the number of touch points that we have with a client:

1   A telephone call, where a meeting is arranged.
2   An e-mail is sent to confirm that meeting.
3   A meeting where it is agreed a proposal will be sent and a follow-up call made.
4   An e-mail is sent to articulate how enjoyable the meeting was and confirm a proposal will be sent shortly.
5   The proposal is sent.
6   On the follow-up call, a second meeting is arranged.
7   An e-mail is sent to confirm that meeting
8   At the second meeting a decision whether to purchase is made

In this second scenario, you have created eight touch points with your potential customer, rather than five. You have caused these to occur without hassling your client or appearing overbearing at any time. The more contacts you have with a customer, the more familiar they become, the more comfortable they feel and the more you allow a relationship to develop.

Far from maximizing the amount of touch points one has with a potential customer, too many possible sales are lost because people do not follow up at all. It seems patently clear that one should not have a meeting or send a proposal and then wait for the customer to get in touch. The fear of failure a customer has regarding a purchase, means that it is often easier for them to do nothing, rather than move the sale forward. Therefore, unless it is an emergency, it is unlikely they will call you, even though they may be receptive when you contact them. Furthermore, in order for a customer to want to do business with you, they have to believe you will deliver on your promises. Part of this is knowing that you care. Failing to follow up demonstrates a degree of indifference, which makes you an unattractive partner.

DEVELOPING RELATIONSHIPS

Successful selling is all about developing relationships. This means any marketing activity which brings you into contact with potential customers should not be wasted.

Whether you make contact with someone via a phone call, at a networking event, or whether they approach you; every person must be followed up and every potential relationship cultivated and developed. Some of these people might make a purchase fairly quickly. Others may make a purchase two years later. A percentage may never buy, but may recommend you to customers who do. Whichever category they ultimately fall into, by following up by e-mail, by telephone, at events and by organizing meetings; once initiated, relationships must be cultivated.

Of course, it takes two people to have a relationship. If someone makes it clear they are not interested in developing one, by not responding to your e-mails or other contacts you make, there is no point in wasting your time. However, when people are happy to continue a dialogue with you, it is precious and should be cherished.

In this way, marketing activities will pay dividends, but only over a long period of time. For example, many people will send out a direct mail piece and receive a few responses. Out of those responses, they may obtain an order. Over time, the other responses are forgotten about. The most costly and hardest part of the sales process is getting on someone's radar and establishing a dialogue with them. Once this has been achieved, it is foolhardy to let that contact disappear.

If you have a robust process, a dialogue will be maintained with the other respondents who did not buy. It may be that this is achieved via e-mail once a quarter with an occasional letter being sent or a phone call being made. It is worthwhile maintaining contact with these people even though they may not require your product or services at the time. These people may come to use your products or services at a later date, or may move to companies who do have a requirement. Staying in touch, in itself, will help to develop trust. The confidence that this gives means that, even if someone never uses your product or services, they may still recommend you to others. Maintaining and developing relationships will produce opportunities that would otherwise be lost.

CONTRIBUTING VALUE

Sometimes, when you make contact, it may be possible to contribute something worthwhile. This might be a useful piece of information. Perhaps you can supply them with a hint or tip that is likely to be beneficial. If you read a relevant article of interest, send it to the person or e-mail them the link. The opportunity to refer business to them may arise. There will be occasions when it will be applicable to send them a discount coupon or an offer on your products or services. Even e-mailing or calling, just to see how someone is getting on, will often be appreciated, because most people do not bother.

Referring business to others and passing on useful information is invaluable, because you will find that many of your contacts will return the favour. Therefore, from these activities alone, you will acquire important knowledge and receive interesting business opportunities. In fact, it is amazing how much business can be generated by continuing relationships that so many let slip away.

- **You can never know too many people.**
- **No business went bankrupt because the people within it had developed too many relationships.**
- **Relationships are absolutely vital, they are the lifeblood of any business.**
- **Fundamentally, all business is; is the relationships you have.**

All business is acquired through a relationship. Moreover, when competitors cut prices or instigate special deals in order to attract your customers, it will be the strength of the relationship that prevents your customers from leaving.

AFTER SALES

Once you have made a sale, following up is essential. If the relationship is more important than the transaction, you do not ignore the relationship once the transaction has been concluded. Instead, you develop the relationship further. Following up after a customer has made a purchase will demonstrate that you care. Assuming they are happy with their purchase, they will be delighted that you are concerned to ensure that this is the case. If, on the other hand, there are any problems, you can deal with them immediately and prevent them from festering. Sometimes, a customer can have an issue about which they do not tell you but relay to friends and colleagues, sullying your reputation. A simple follow-up will stop this happening, while giving you the opportunity to put things right.

If you have only a few customers, following up should be easy. It may be, in a bigger organization, that you employ account managers to remain in touch with customers. Even with thousands of customers, modern technology will allow an automated process to be put in place whereby intuitive software can track the purchases people make and send them relevant offers and advice.

KEEPING IN TOUCH

Ultimately, we must keep in touch with everyone: existing customers, previous customers and those who might become customers in the future. There is so much value in the contacts we make. However, because people do not store these in an appropriate database and follow them up diligently, they are literally throwing money down the drain.

> • How many lapsed customers have you telephoned or written to, who could possibly become a customer again?
> • How many existing customers will be retained and purchase more, if you just stay in contact with them occasionally?
> • How many recommendations or referrals from customers are you missing out on because you are 'out of sight, out of mind?'
> • How many contacts have you had over the past one, two or three years who, if you had just stayed in contact, would also have recommended you to others or eventually become customers as well?

The fact is, the cost of acquiring a customer is continually increasing. Therefore, in order to be as profitable as possible, you must maximize the contacts and relationships that you have.

In order to do this effectively, you must genuinely care about your relationships and try and give value when possible. People should not only hear from you when you are trying to sell something. By developing meaningful relationships, you will build a robust business. This is because you will cultivate a loyal contact list and customer base who will not readily switch to competitors.

Epilogue

YOUR FIRST 12 STEPS TO SALES THERAPY®

- Sales Therapy® is a philosophy.
- It is an approach to selling, in a world, where relationships **must** come first.
- It is a way of being commercially successful, while working with the highest standards of morality and integrity.
- It is **'winning customers by caring'**.

This book is the start of a journey. Whether your business consists of only yourself, or if you employ many people, it is the beginning of building a sales-centric organization; that is, an organization built in a way that attracts business and is best placed to gain business. This is of course, fundamental.

- Every business is a sales organization.
- Without sales there are no customers.
- Without customers, there is no business.

The journey will not be easy. If it were, everyone would be successful and that is certainly not the case. As you embark down this road, it is worth remembering something Winston Churchill once said:

> *'Success is not final, failure is not fatal; it is the courage to continue that counts.'*

Perhaps the hardest part of embarking on a new adventure is the beginning. Therefore, I have listed a first 12 steps to help you on your way.

There is more support available and it would be a privilege to share in your experience.

Please visit www.salestherapy.com to gain access to a host of materials and ideas to make the process easier.

Your first 12 steps

1   Make sure you have clarity in your sales message and understand your buyer's motivations. In order to do this you must undertake a Problem Map™. Ask yourself what problems you solve and what the resulting issues caused by those problems are.

2   Identify who your key customers are. This is done by examining your Problem Map™ and asking yourself who is likely to have the problems and who are the secondary groups that may also be affected.

3   Create additional Problem Maps™ for any specific customer types, or situations, which you have established.

4   Answer the key question, 'Why am I uniquely placed to solve the problem?' Examine:
   • the market – what others do;
   • yourself – what you do and any particular relevant expertise you have; and
   • your customers – are there particular types of customer or particular geographical areas where you could offer something special.

5   Evaluate your product or service against the potential risks for your customer. Take into account:
   • cost;
   • the conditions necessary to ensure your solution works; and
   • your customer's reputation and what others, around them, may think.

Having evaluated these risks, build in reassurances for your customer.

6   Decide on your ESP. Ask yourself:
   • What do the problems that you solve mean emotionally?
   • What emotions do you want your customer to experience?
7   Benchmark your ESP against everything you do, for example:
   • your logo and corporate colours;
   • the way you and your staff dress;
   • the service your customers receive; and
   • your materials, e.g. websites, brochures, etc.
8   Examine your financial goals and customer base and decide on your sales targets for the year.
9   Determine the routes to market that you will utilize. Remember to take an integrated approach.
10 Develop a compelling narrative.
11 Identify the small steps and commitments customers can take on their journey moving from prospect to customer.
12 Get out there, utilizing the techniques contained in this book.

These 12 steps are merely suggestions to get you going. They are the start of a continuing process. There is no one panacea for achieving success. It is a series of steps that, if taken, will pull you closer to the goal.

Index